*The First Two Years*
*of*
*Marriage*

# The First Two Years of Marriage

*Foundations for a Life Together*

THOMAS N. HART

*and*

KATHLEEN FISCHER HART

 **paulist press**   *new york/ramsey*

Library of Congress Catalog Card Number: 83-60375

ISBN: 0-8091-2553-6

Published by Paulist Press
545 Island Road, Ramsey, N.J. 07446

Printed and bound in the United States of America

# *Contents*

# *Introduction*

ONCE THERE WAS A POOR MAN who left his village, weary of his life, longing for a place where he could escape all the struggles of this earth. He set out in search of a magical city, the heavenly city of his dreams, where all things would be perfect. He walked all day and by dusk found himself in a deep forest, where he decided to spend the night. He ate the crust of bread he had brought, then knelt to pray. Placing his shoes in the center of the path, he said: "Lord God, please point my shoes in the direction of the magical city I seek." Then he went to sleep.

The next morning he got up, gave thanks to the Lord of the universe, and started again on his way in the direction that his shoes pointed. For a second time he walked all day, and toward evening finally saw the magical city in the distance. It was not as large as he had expected. As he got closer, it looked curiously familiar. But he pressed on, found a street much like his own, knocked on a familiar door, and

1

greeted the family he found there. Then his eyes were opened and he exclaimed: "I am home again! But it is as if I am seeing the place for the first time!" And there he lived ever after, in the magical city of his dreams.

This story from rabbinic literature illustrates the truth that governs our approach to giving marriage enrichment events. Our conviction is that there are resources deep in a marriage that have never been tapped, hidden potential for laughter, warmth, and closeness that is lying unused. We all dream of other marriages, magical ones which are the way they are supposed to be, not realizing that there is an abundance of magic lying dormant in our present marriage, waiting for someone to awaken it. So on marriage enrichment days, we invite couples to rediscover themselves and each other, in somewhat the same way they did when they first fell in love with each other.

This book is written in that spirit, and addressed specifically to couples in the first two years of marriage. Perhaps you find yourselves in a situation where the first luster of love has worn off, problems have arisen, and you are wondering if the whole thing was a big mistake. Perhaps your marriage is going well in many respects, but less well in a few others. Perhaps you are right at the beginning and would welcome some suggestions on what to watch for. Or perhaps you are beyond the first two years, but feel you still need to develop some of the fundamentals. This book is written for couples in all of these situations.

The first two years of marriage are a crucial period. They are foundational. The arrangements that a couple makes in this initial period, and the ways they develop for dealing with all that is involved in married living, will determine to a great extent how the marriage will play itself out for years to come. But this initial period is not only important. It is usually difficult. Living so closely with someone, even someone you love very much, is a great challenge and involves not a few surprises. The incidence of divorce is very high in the first two years, among the highest in the whole span of marriage. Some couples are already separated in the first few months, after having been the best of friends for years. Everyone is amazed, most of all the couples themselves. This book is written to help prevent that kind of tragedy. We treat the typical struggles of the first two years and offer some strategies for dealing with them. We develop both the attitudes and the basic skills needed to sustain an intimate relationship. Our treatment is set in the context of Christian faith.

As Christians we believe that God wants our marriages to succeed. We believe that God wants us both to love and to be loved deeply, and to be happy in this kind of living. In fact, the New Testament tells us that when a married couple lives in love, they become the embodiment of the kind of love God has for all persons. Marriage is a great vocation, and God's fidelity to us in our adventure of living it is our indispensable support.

This book comes out of our counseling work with individuals and couples, our experience in giving marriage enrichment events for groups of couples, and the lived experience of our own marriage. Probably the best approach to the book is for you to read it together as a couple and to discuss it chapter by chapter in the light of your own relationship. Exercises have been placed at the end of each chapter to help you apply the material to your own marriage. Suggestions for further reading are also offered at the end of the book.

We want to express our thanks to our professional colleagues who were good enough to read the manuscript and offer many helpful suggestions on it. We are grateful likewise to the many couples who shared their stories with us. We have changed their names and some details of their stories out of respect for their desire to be anonymous. Because of their gift to us, our book reflects something of the height and the depth, the length and the breadth of Christian marriage, and the beauty of the human spirit.

# 1
# *Expectations*

BILL AND CINDY HAD A DREAM about how their marriage was going to be. Bill had started dreaming about marriage already in high school, when he was experiencing loneliness and all relationships seemed superficial and phony. Someday he would have a very special friend and lover, and they would do everything together. He had visions of laughter and much physical affection, of sitting close and watching TV in the evenings, or just talking, of making love often and with great tenderness. He would share all of himself, honestly and without fear, and so would she. They would be intensely interested in one another, and feel, probably for the first time in their lives, completely happy.

Cindy's dream was similar. All her life she had longed for someone to whom she could be special, who would treat her with respect and be gentle and tender to her. She had visions of going places and doing exciting things with her husband, of being told frequently that she was beautiful and that she looked nice, of really being Number One in somebody's life. Her vision of marriage with Bill did not include fighting. Her parents had fought a great deal, but she saw that as her mother's fault and she did not plan on being like her mother. And she and Bill had a very good record on that score in their year and a half of going together. Bill and Cindy shared their dreams, and found that they agreed. Anticipation ran high.

The disillusionment that came in the first year of marriage was awful. Cindy cried a lot, and Bill walked with a heavy heart. Both had outside jobs that first year. Bill would come home stressed out, looking for warmth and affection from Cindy. But Cindy would be tired too, and, if things had not gone well during the day, irritable besides. Bill would want to share, but Cindy showed less interest than before. She accused him of not listening to her. They watched TV all right, but the warmth was missing. Bill would be looking forward to ending the day with lovemaking, but Cindy seemed more concerned with getting a good night's sleep. It bothered Bill that Cindy showed so little sexual interest in him. What surprised Cindy was that Bill was no longer as affectionate as he used to be, no longer looked at her in the same way or told her she was beautiful. He didn't embrace her as often, and failed to notice many of the little things she did to make their home more attractive. He came on, it seemed, only when he wanted sex.

There were other problems too. The cost of renting and furnishing a place and keeping two cars going took all the money they had, and there were no trips and few dinners out. They had much difficulty finding other couples they both enjoyed being with, and who seemed to be comfortable with both of them. And Cindy had trouble getting along with Bill's mother, who showed them a lot of attention and freely shared her advice with Cindy about what Bill needed and about how to manage a household. Bill was not particularly fond of his mother, but he tended to defend her against Cindy's criticisms. The result of all these unexpected developments was a lot of arguing in that first year, and much more silence than either of them was comfortable with. Cindy could hardly believe that her marriage showed some of the same patterns her parents' marriage did, and she was doing some of the very things she hated her mother for doing. Bill, for his part, was haunted with the question: Have I made a big mistake?

Bill and Cindy's experience is not at all unusual. Probably most couples expect more of marriage than it can deliver, and have to undergo a painful disillusionment. We need our dreams, or we might settle for less than we could have. But in the area of romantic love especially, an unreality can creep into our dreaming, setting us up for acute disappointment. Bill's and Cindy's dreams flow from deep longings in the human heart. All of us want more intensity and excitement in life, and more love. But these longings of the heart may more suggest what awaits us in the next life than what we will find in marriage. Perhaps if we look at some of the most common unrealistic expectations for marriage, and revise them, we will feel better about what we actually have in marriage and see more possibilities in it.

1. **We will do everything together.** This might be nice, but it cannot be. My interests are bound to diverge from yours, and yours from mine, in various areas. I will want male companionship at times, and you female, without each other's company. We will not share all the same activities because we do not share all the same interests. In fact, in the same way that we used to escape together from the routine of our individual lives, we will probably want to escape singly at times from the routine of being together.

2. We will always feel the same way about things. About some things, yes. About other things, no. We are unique individuals. The families in which we were raised were different "culturally," and we are stamped by those differences. When we marry, two "cultures" come together under the same roof. Seeing eye to eye with one another may be as difficult at times as it is for Israelis and Arabs or Westerners and Orientals. Values are different. Customs are different. You make little of birthdays; to me, my birthday is the most important day of the year. You express anger openly and strongly; I avoid conflict and hold angry feelings in. You are physically affectionate; I was raised in a home in which we very rarely touched each other. Each of us brings a different pair of glasses and a different set of habits to the unfolding drama of life. The key is going to be learning to live and let live, accepting and blessing our diversity, and not trying to establish who is right and who is wrong.

3. You will always be intensely interested in me, and I in you. One of the marvelous things about being in love is that this is the way things are for a while. I *am* intensely interested in you, and you in me. You may be the first person I have ever known in such depth. You are most certainly the first person who has ever found me so fascinating. And when we are together, it is usually a special time, a temporary escape from our humdrum separate existences at home, at school, or at work. But we get used to each other. If we are not careful, we may even begin to take each other for granted. In the best of circumstances, I hear you say the same things many times over, and you reach a stage where you can give my whole speech on any subject if I provide but the cue. Each of us will continue to give birth to new things as our lives unfold, and it would be a shame not to notice. But there will never be so much so fast as there was at the

beginning. So we had better be sure we have each other's attention before beginning to speak.

4. **There will be a lot of sex and warm physical closeness.** If you are driving down the freeway and the couple in the car ahead of you is sitting so close that you wonder if they are one person or two, they are probably not married. This is not because married couples do not love each other, but only because they are a little more relaxed about it most of the time. Being together has become a way of life. And sex is just a part of it. Somebody has to go out and buy food once in a while, and walk the dog. Even the intensity of the first sexual encounters is a little hard to sustain. For sex lives in a total context and varies with feelings and energy. It is almost impossible to have a very accurate picture of all this before marriage. But one can safely expect that things will not be as expected.

5. **You will meet all my deeper needs, and I yours.** Actually, the first part of this expectation is the more common one, and it is not fully conscious. So when I feel misunderstood in the marriage, or still lonely at times, or unable to get you interested in my favorite activity, I feel as if you have let me down. But am I being fair? Did you promise that you would meet all my deeper needs? Could you possibly? No. Each of the parties to a marriage needs to live in a larger social world and to draw on resources outside the marriage, as well as inside, for life and love. When we try to get our mates to do it all, we imprison and drain them, and sooner or later they will probably run for their lives.

6. **The character defects I now see in you will disappear under the influence of my love.** This would be wonderful. But it is most unlikely. Alcoholics do not usually recover by marriage. Neatniks remain neatniks. Those who

tend to be lazy are not suddenly energized. And moody folks tend, alas, to remain moody. In fact, you may have seen less of your mate's undesirable qualities during courtship, when both of you were on your good behavior.

People do change in life, especially if they work at it and are loved well. Marriage is a growthful state. But if you want a sense of how hard it is to change habits that are rooted deeply in our personalities, look at yourself and how many years you have struggled to change some of the things you don't like about yourself. Most likely, the "character defects" you see in your mate will persist a good long time, even if the two of you genuinely love one another.

7. **The details of our living will fall naturally into place.** Alas, it is precisely the details that stick in the machinery. It is the wet towel in the middle of the bathroom floor, the near empty gas tank, and the dirty dishes in the sink that test the durability of the bond. If you would close your mouth when you chew, refrain from profanity, and close the door quietly when you come and go, we would have no problems. If we could agree on the arrangement of the furniture, a comfortable temperature, and a proper time to go to bed, we might make fifty years. It is precisely the details that call for tolerance and negotiation.

8. **We will probably never fight.** We know a couple who were terribly surprised, even shocked, when they had their first fight. They had never fought before they got married, and were sure they never would. And their first fight was not a quiet little one; it was a noisy big one that left them nursing their wounds and still arguing in their heads in separate beds.

Why the dreadful eruption? They had not dealt with occasions as they arose, but allowed irritations to build up.

Each was feeling, below the level of immediate offenses, some painful disillusionments with how their life together was actually shaping up. And they were as yet unskilled at expressing negative feelings and working through differences. Do good couples fight? Yes, in some way or other. Some have dramatic flareups, go apart and think about it, and come back and make up, closer for the conflict. Others deal with their differences in quieter exchanges and get the message just as well. What is important is that differences be dealt with. It is better to "fight it out" in some way than to try to bury things. Even between those who love each other deeply and truly, anger and conflict are inevitable. They can be very growthful.

9. **We enter this marriage with pretty much the same expectations.** Actually we do not. We have some of the same expectations, and we have talked about them. But we have many different ones too, unspoken because largely unconscious. A man's sexism, for instance, is usually unconscious; it is in the culture, and he has simply absorbed it. And culture, as we have said, is the key to understanding this whole matter. Both parties to a marriage were raised in a family "culture," and from it they learned many things about what a man's and woman's role are, how the house is kept up, children raised, time spent separately or together. Many of these expectations will appear in the present marriage only as circumstances unfold. They cannot all be declared beforehand because they are simply taken for granted.

There is another unsettling thing about expectations. They are fluid, and some of them change even in the first two years. A man may have entered marriage thinking he wanted children, and his feelings change. A woman may have thought she wanted to be mother and homemaker, only to find her inclinations moving toward more education or a job outside the home. In this respect, marriage is like a young sapling which has to bend with the wind and keep adapting to changing conditions. The key to longevity in marriage too is flexibility.

10. **Our marriage will be different from all the bad ones we have seen.** It probably will, being both better and worse. It could be much better than many, but that depends on a lot of hard work and some favorable breaks rather than on the simple fact that it is we, not they. All those other folks too started out very much in love and full of dreams. Human sinfulness and limitation wore them down. And these things, like the air we breathe, are in every household.

Where do all these unrealistic expectations come from? They come partly from the deep longings of the human heart, as we have said. They are born also of the experience of falling in love. Falling in love is wonderful, and much of the world's great poetry and music have been spun from the experience. People in love need no one and nothing else. There is discovery, excitement, and a feeling of fullness. Here is someone I can talk with, be genuinely myself with, be understood and accepted by. Here at last is a friend and lover. My world is tremendously expanded, my daily life marvelously enlivened. Being apart leaves a terrible ache, and we languish and yearn to be together again. When together, I am reflected back to myself with warmth and enthusiasm, and I can hardly help feeling whole. And I suddenly have something to do in life: to love and be loved by you. There is someone to go places with, someone to hold and be held by, someone with whom to be lifted above the dullness and difficulties of life. For a time, the experience is all-absorbing.

Unfortunately, it does not last. What is substantial in it

can endure, but there are elements of unreality in it which must gradually yield to the harsher light of day. When we are in love, more sober folk indulge us with patience. Psychologists warn us that we project a lot. We impose an idealized image on our partners so that we cannot see them as they are. The wisdom of the ages tells us that love is blind, and people who are in love are often "madly" in love. But reality gradually regains the ascendency, and we discover that our partner is an ordinary mortal, and a sinner at that. If this happens after marriage, the awakening is an added part of the difficulty of adjusting. If we have been together long enough before marriage that we are no longer in love, at least not so madly, the adjustment will be easier.

Loving someone over the years is a very different matter from being in love. It is much less an emotional state, much more a choice. Falling in love is something that *happens* to a person; loving someone is something a person *chooses* to do or not do. And so, in most marriages, there dawns a morning when one finds oneself in sober reflection. One man we know put it down this way in his journal.

I know you pretty well now. I used to think I understood you completely; now I wonder if I understand you very much at all. There are many things I can share with you, but some I find it hard to. I think the same holds true for you, so our communication has its gaps.

I haven't gotten all I hoped for when I married you. There are some things you just cannot be for me. There are also some things about you that really bother me. I wasn't fully aware of them when I married you. Sometimes I look around and wonder if I wouldn't be happier with someone else. That is probably an illusion though. And I realize that you could say all the same things about me.

I am going to go on loving you. You are a good per-

son, and I love many things about you. You have loved
me, as best you can. I need that. I think you need my love
too. I know I have a lot to learn about loving, about getting outside myself, about acceptance. I'd really like to do
it with you. We've shared so much. I know that any marriage I would get into would eventually come down to
this same thing: the choice to love or to move out in quest
of greener pastures. I am going to work at the relationship we've got. I'm going to keep trying to listen and understand, to meet your needs insofar as I can, to be there
for you. You can count on me.

Lord, help me to do this. Teach me to love Ginger
the way you do.

At this, the marriage takes a large growth-step forward.
It becomes mature. As the years go on, it will keep coming
into question from time to time. The commitment will have
to be made over again, especially at critical junctures. From a
religious standpoint, these crises or passages are moments
when the mystery of death/resurrection is experienced. The
marriage as it was dies, and it rises again to new life. It takes
courage and surrender to go through it, and hope in God's
power to regenerate and renew. But this is the law of
growth, the only access to deeper, richer levels of living.

If the ideas with which this chapter opened are unrealistic expectations of marriage, what might we more realistical-
ly expect? Perhaps some metaphors can help us get at the
reality of it.

1. The German philosopher Nietzsche mused that marriage is a long conversation. So marry a friend, he said.

2. Marriage is not gazing at one another, but looking
outward together in the same direction.

3. Marriage is a long walk two people take together. Sometimes the terrain is very interesting, sometimes rather dull. At times the walk is arduous, for both persons or for one. Sometimes the conversation is lively; at other times, there is not much to say. The travelers do not know exactly where they are going, nor when they will arrive. But they share everything they have. And they find that it is a lot more fun, and also a great help, to walk with a companion rather than alone.

4. Marriage is a continual compromise, with life and with each other.

5. Marriage is a covenant of love and fidelity, in good times and in bad. It mirrors the covenant of love and fidelity, in good times and in bad, which God has with each human being. This is the New Testament's metaphor for marriage.

If I am married, and find myself with an expectation which is not being met, what can I do? I can examine it and see if it might fall into the category of the unrealistic. If so, I can quietly let go of it. If it seems realistic to me, I can share it with my mate. I make my needs and wants known. Sometimes this is all it takes to make new things happen. Sometimes the situation is more difficult.

A woman came for marriage counseling who had been married some fifteen years. She was deeply frustrated because her husband would not share his feelings with her, but would only talk about his business, the weather, and other matters of fact. He loved her. But no matter how hard she tried, and she had been doing it for fifteen years, she could not get him to share his feelings. Deeply frustrated, she had finally moved out, and then come for counseling. A few joint sessions with both husband and wife convinced us that even though the man had good will, given his background, his habits, and his age, this man was simply not going to become a sharer of feelings. So we asked the woman to come in alone, and we reviewed her options with her: (1) She could leave this man and look for someone who would share his feelings with her. (2) She could go back to him and keep working on him (though fifteen years of this had been fruitless). (3) She could go back to him and love him as he was. But if she chose this last, it would mean renouncing the deepest dream she had had for her marriage.

Those three options are always the options, in one form or another, in situations of dissatisfaction. (1) You can leave the situation and look for a better one. (2) You can remain in the situation and keep striving for what you want. (3) You can remain in the situation, accepting it, and letting part of your dream go.

The woman in the story chose the last option, because she could not conceive of living the rest of her life without this man, whom she loved, and because she realized that she was not going to change this thing in him. And the sequel was a happy one. When she stopped pressuring him to deliver what he scarcely could, he began to show her love in new an unexpected ways. In making the choice she did, she died a painful death, a death to her own expectations. And they both rose to new life.

## EXERCISES

Each exercise begins as you go off by yourself with a piece of paper, do some reflecting, and make some notes for yourself. It ends in some sharing with your mate, who has made similar preparations.

1. What were your expectations in each of the following areas when you came into the marriage?

   | finances | sex | leisure |
   |----------|---------|---------------|
   | roles | friends | religion |
   | in-laws | children | communication |
   | | | conflict |

   What are your expectations, hopes, and dreams now in the light of experience?

2. What is an expectation you may have to give up in this marriage as you have come to know it? What effect might giving it up have on you and your mate? If you would like, spend some time in prayer, asking God to strengthen you for the death you would have to die to do so.

3. What are some good things that have befallen you in this marriage which you did *not* expect?

# 2

# *Communication*

WHEN TONY AND SUE CAME IN for counseling, they had been married five years and had two children. But things were not going at all well. At a recent workshop for couples, the two of them had been asked to recall one or two of the peak experiences of their marriage, and Tony could not think of any. He wondered if he was just so angry that his recall of anything good was blocked. As we talked, the roots of the anger were gradually uncovered. Tony summed up the problem this way: "Sue never understands me, and so she always reacts in the wrong way. But you know, the reason she doesn't understand me is that I have never really let her know me." Sue chimed in and said: "Everything he said is true. What's worse, he doesn't understand me either. And that's my fault, because I've held back too. So you can imagine what our guessing-game interaction is like." They went on to say that it had been like this from the beginning.

This clear analysis of their problem, offered by the couple themselves, set the agenda for counseling. The task was to assist them to begin to talk to one another about what was going on deep inside, to open out their inner worlds to one another. The heart of that was to get them expressing how they felt about themselves, each other, and the myriad situations of their lives. Tony admitted that the reason he held himself in was that he did not like himself very much, and he found it much easier to remain crouched behind his wall sniping at Sue than to come out from behind it and let her see who he was. To do the latter would be to make himself vulnerable, to admit hurt, weakness, inadequacy, and need, and to put the truth in Sue's hands for her to deal with. That required a degree of courage he had long been unable to muster.

We talk in Christian terms of the gift of the self. In marriage, that is what two Christians pledge to one another. It is *the* great gift of love. Many married people stay with one another and serve each other in many ways. But this is not yet the gift of the *self*, which can only be given if one is willing to open one's heart to the other. One can do many external deeds of love and still hold back the really precious gift, the inner self. This gift can be given only through communication. It costs, like all of the better gifts. But union between two persons is hardly possible if they have not let each other into their inner worlds. This always involves the disclosure of feelings.

Some feelings are harder to communicate than others. Some people, for some reason, find it next to impossible to say "I love you." Many people, especially men, find it difficult to admit their fears, their sense of failure, or their sadness. Some find it hard to affirm others, to give positive feedback. Husbands stop telling their wives that they are beautiful, saying, "She already knows that," or "It would go to her head." We have yet to meet someone who does not need to be told the good things over and over (and even then still doubts it), or whose head is in much danger of an over-swell from too much affirmation. But there is another reason why people hold in their feelings in marriage. They care about their mates and do not want to hurt them. So they do not express dissatisfaction, irritation, or any other uncomfortable feelings.

What happens in an intimate relationship when uncomfortable feelings are held in? Terrible outbursts from time to time, when feelings reach the breaking point. A note on the kitchen table announcing the divorce. Or, in milder forms, sarcasm, silence, and various forms of subtle punishment. One thing is certain. If people cannot deal with their anger, they cannot be intimate either. You either have a relationship in which there are angry exchanges at times and warm closeness at others (often shortly after the angry exchange), or you have a relationship in which all is smooth on the surface but the psychological distance is unbridged. In these latter relationships there are several forbidden subjects and an abundance of silence.

In intimate relationships, communication is the foundational skill. There is none more basic. It is the indispensable condition of union. It is the key to resolving conflicts. It is the only way two people can continue growing together, or even living together.

The question is: How do you do it? It is an art, and it takes time to cultivate. The following are eleven hints to point the way.

1. **Use I-statements rather than You-statements.** Talk about yourself rather than your mate. Don't say things like, "*You* never care about anybody but yourself," or "*You* think you know everything all the time," or "*You* never do

anything around here." Say instead, "*I* often feel lonely," or "Sometimes *I* feel put down by things you say," or "*I* feel overburdened with household chores and sometimes *I* resent it because it doesn't seem fair to me." Talk about yourself, in other words, and your feelings, in response to concrete behaviors of your mate. Do that instead of making judgments about your mate ("You're always flirting"; "You're so damn sure about everything") or giving commands ("Get out of here"; "Why don't you loosen up once in a while?").

The approach we are suggesting is risky because it exposes you. But it has many distinct advantages. It does not make your mate so defensive, and so it gives you a better chance of getting a hearing and an honest response. It lets your mate in on your inner world, and so reveals important information. It does not pronounce judgment about who is wrong, but leaves the question open. For instance, if I am bothered by the way you socialize at parties, it may indeed be your fault. But it could just as well be mine. Maybe I am very insecure, and cling too much, and am very easily threatened and jealous. Maybe I misinterpret what you are doing. If I find you overly emotional, it may be that you are. But it may also be that I am emotionally repressed and uncomfortable with the expression of feelings, or simply that I feel inadequate to meeting the needs you make known to me. When I stay with my own feelings, owning them and letting you know them, I let you know me and I leave the question open about who should do what. We can work on that together. "I feel uncomfortable around your dad" is not yet a comment about your dad, still less about you. So far, it is just an informative comment about me.

Talking about your mate is legitimate to this extent: As far as possible, tie your feeling statements to your mate's concrete *behaviors*. "When you come in without saying hello, I feel unloved." "I start to feel insecure when I see you having a good time with another man." You are talking here just about concrete *behaviors,* externally observable. You are not guessing at your mate's *feelings* or *intentions,* which are hidden from view.

There are four basic I-statements which carry most of the weight in an intimate relationship. They are: (1) I think, (2) I feel, (3) I want, and (4) I need. All of them are positive steps in self-assertion and indicate an underlying self-respect. All of them make me vulnerable to you. They do not state what is right, nor do they make a demand. They simply tell you who I am and what is going on with me right now. If you are willing to make a similar self-revelation, we have the materials for really learning to care for one another.

2. **Express feelings rather than thoughts.** Not that it is bad to express thoughts. There is plenty of scope for those too. But our feelings reveal more of who we are. One can sit for an entire course before many professors, and know a good deal of their thought and almost nothing of who they are. A wife expressed this eloquently once, saying that everything her husband said to her could be said on television. He was an engineer, and lived much more in the realm of thought than of feeling. He was not untalkative, but she was always left wondering what was going on inside. It is in expressing our feelings that we give the gift of the self. That was the gift she was still waiting for.

People sometimes hide their feelings behind their thoughts. "A woman's place is in the home" is an apparent statement of principle, but it may be a man's way of saying that he feels he has failed as a provider if his wife takes a job outside the home, or that he fears he will lose her if she has much occasion to be with other men. Those are feelings. "Should" statements can also be masks. "You should enjoy sex" is probably best translated "I enjoy sex," or "I feel inadequate as a lover when you don't seem to enjoy sex, or hurt when you turn me down." In more open communication, people just talk about their feelings, not about the eternal order of things (as they see it), or the common sense truths embraced by all (but you). Most of our feelings, after all, come out of our cultural relativity.

Some people are not very aware of their feelings. You cannot communicate what you do not know. To develop a greater awareness of feelings, it is a helpful exercise to go inside yourself from time to time during the day, inquiring what you are feeling right now. Watch the variations in typical situations: talking with your child, talking with the boss, hearing the phone ring, approaching the front door at home, waking up in the morning, watching TV at night, going about your daily work, getting into bed at night. Move gradually from becoming more aware of feelings to becoming more expressive of them.

3. **Listen attentively without interrupting.** Good communication requires more than good talking. It demands good listening too. Listening is difficult. It requires setting other things aside, even the ruminations of the mind. It is especially hard when we do not like what we are hearing, or when we think we have heard it all before. One of the things a marriage counselor does most frequently is stop married partners from interrupting each other, suggesting instead a three-step process which can revolutionize the way they talk to each other: (a) listen without interrupting; (b) say back what you heard, and check it out; (c) respond to it.

In poor communication, the listeners are working on their responses instead of listening, and cut in to make them as soon as they are ready. In the approach suggested here, you have to listen closely or you will not be able to say back what you heard. This is how you make sure you got the message.

There are often surprises here, as the original speaker makes the necessary corrections. Then you can respond. This may seem cumbersome and time-consuming. But if you really get your mate's message, and respond to it rather than to something else, you end up saving time. And your mate has the gratifying feeling of being heard, even if you end up differing. If two people are in the habit of interrupting each other as they argue back and forth, the entire time is probably being wasted. Neither is listening. Neither is open. Nothing is being produced except more bad feeling.

4. **Check out what you see and hear.** Part of this is summarizing what you hear your mate saying and asking if that is the message. It keeps the conversation on track. But there are other parts to this checking out too. Listen for the feelings behind the words, and check those out. Listen for anger and frustration. Listen for loneliness. Listen for fear. And test what you think you hear, saying, for example, "You sound weary," or, "You sound as if this is really hard for you to tell me." This approach is especially useful with people who do not express feelings directly, but prefer to make statements of fact, pronounce judgments of good and bad, and give direct or indirect commands. You cannot get them to play by your rules. If you say, "Don't make judgments; tell me your feelings," you have given them a command instead of expressing your frustration and leaving them free. Even if they persist in their usual ways, you can listen for the feelings behind the words, and check those out.

Checking out can be useful outside of times of conversation. You come home, and seem tired, discouraged, or distant. But I am not sure. Mostly you are silent. If I want to relate to you appropriately—giving you space, encouraging you, or inviting you to unburden yourself—I have to know what you are feeling. I can ask the open question, "How are you doing?" Or I can check out my impressions: "You seem distant." Or, "You look as if you had a hard day."

Such an approach invites mates to express themselves. The ideal situation would be that they would volunteer this information, and ask for what they need. But the situation is not always ideal.

5. **Avoid mind-reading.** Mind-reading is the attempt to reach inside the sanctuary of the other person's psyche and declare what is going on there. You tell others what they are feeling or what their motives are. "You're saying that because you're jealous." "You're just telling me what you think I want to hear." This kind of statement almost always gets an angry reaction. It deserves it. The statement is a violation of the other's privacy, and what is alleged is often inaccurate besides. We have *impressions* of other people's feelings, and *hunches* about their motives. It is legitimate to inquire. It is also all right to voice our impressions, if we do it tentatively, with recognition of our uncertainty. Mind-reading is another matter. It is a violation of the person. It shows disrespect for that person's integrity, destroys trust, and invites retaliation.

6. **Make your needs known.** Sometimes those needs are general: "I need about half an hour's space when I get home from work before I can face any new challenges." "I need relief from child care at least one day a week." Sometimes they are particular: "I need a hug." "I need to get away some weekend soon."

A couple came for counseling. The problem they brought was that the husband was angry much of the time. What came to light was that he expected his wife to anticipate his needs and take care of them, and when she did not, he got angry. He expected her to know when he needed space, and not to talk to him then. He expected her to know when he needed affection, and to be affectionate then. When she guessed wrong and acted unsuitably, he was angry. This is an extreme form of a common fallacy: "If you really loved me, you would know what I am feeling and what I need." Not so. All of us are unfamiliar territory, often even to ourselves, certainly to others. Our only hope of getting our needs met is to be assertive in declaring them. They will not always get met, of course, because others have their needs too and some limitations in their ability to meet ours. But if needs are declared, they can at least be negotiated.

7.   **Learn your mate's language of love.** All of us have a language in which we like to be told that we are loved. And one person's language differs from another's. What tells Randy that he is loved is a massage by Betty. But what tells Betty that she is loved is not a return massage by Randy, but just being held by him. What told your mother that your father was sorry was a single red rose, but what tells *your* wife you are sorry is not a rose at all but an apology and an explanation of what was going on inside you at the time of the incident. A woman might express her love by keeping a very clean house, but what would actually speak love to her husband would be her relaxing more with him.

There is usually a lot of love in the first two years of marriage, but sometimes it is spoken in your own language rather than your mate's, and so it does not have much impact. The trick is to learn your mate's language and to speak that. One very ironic situation of our acquaintance was that of a couple who differed in how they wanted to be treated when they were sick. She liked people to come into her room, freshen the air, bring her some orange juice, ask her how she was, and leave some flowers behind. He liked to be left completely alone so he could sleep. So when she was sick, he left her alone. And when he was sick, she visited him often and did all kinds of nice things for him. It took them a while to learn each other's language. It usually does. The Golden Rule here is "Do unto others as they would have you do unto them."

8. **Avoid the words "always" and "never."** This is an easy one to understand, but a hard one to do. "Always" and "never" are very tempting words, especially when you are angry. "You *never* listen." "You're *always* complaining." "You *never* want to do anything but watch TV." Because they are exaggerations, they provoke anger and invite a quick denial. And so the point is missed. Wouldn't "sometimes" be a better word than "always," more accurate and easier for the other person to hear? Then there is "often," and, when you really want to be emphatic, "usually." Never use "never."

9. **Avoid name-calling.** Names usually come into the game in the heat of anger. They hurt (which is why they are used). They stick. That is the problem. The fight ends, you make up, and things are supposed to be all right again. But your mate cannot forget that name you called her. Did you really mean that? If you didn't mean it, why did you say it? You have unwittingly planted a weed, and weeds are very hard to eradicate.

A couple once agreed in marriage counseling to just two contracts with one another. They would not read each other's minds and they would not call each other names. Seventy-five percent of their wrangling dropped away.

10. **Deal with painful situations as they arise.** Have you had the experience of setting off an angry tirade by some simple slip-up, like being five minutes late to pick up your mate? There has probably been some gunnysacking going on, and the sack has just burst. You take it over the head not just for the present offense but for several others stretching back over weeks and months. You didn't know your mate was carrying all this around. You can't even remember the incidents they refer to.

If couples would be close, they must learn to deal with anger honestly and constructively. That means handling it by occasions, not allowing it to build. There is no point in try-ing not to hurt your mate with the bad news that you did not like something. You will harm your mate more in the long run if you hold these things back. You can soften the pain by telling the truth with love each time. That way you avoid the big outburst with white-hot anger, exaggerated statements, name-calling, and sometimes physical violence.

11. **Make time for talk that goes beyond practical problems.** Most couples manage to get the day-to-day prob-lems solved. They communicate enough to get the bills paid, the food bought, the baby taken care of, the guests enter-tained, the car fixed. But many couples gradually neglect talking about themselves. The very thing that made the courting period such a deeply happy time, talking about you and about me and about us, gets pushed from the center to the periphery and sometimes dies out altogether. We make love less frequently, and I notice it, but I don't say anything. We do more things separately, and talk about them less. I go to work and muse a lot on the general drift of my life, but I keep these thoughts and feelings to myself. You go off to be with your parents. We keep solving the day-to-day problems,

but we do not talk about *ourselves.* And both of us notice in our interaction a growing distance and irritability.

Marriage Encounter has a simple idea to keep marriages going and growing. Each day the couple write each other a short letter, no more than ten minutes' worth, on some subject that draws out feelings. Some couples accomplish the same purpose in other ways. They keep an agreement to do something together one night a week, to be by themselves and talk about things that are important to each of them. It may be a dinner, or it may just be a walk. Other couples commit themselves to a weekend away every few months. These exercises in deliberate cultivation of the relationship are vital. Often all that is needed is to remove the obstacles, the challenges that ordinary living throws in the way of deeper communication. If we can free ourselves from these regularly, the deeper currents can keep flowing and joining. There is an amazing power of resurrection in marital relationships if they are not neglected too long. The coals may seem a little quiet at times, but don't call the fire out. Couples who make a little time and tend the embers see some amazing things happen. The habit of doing this needs to be formed in the first two years. We offer further suggestions on it in Chapter 5.

Communication is the foundational skill, and the key to all the rest of the elements that build a marriage. It is learned over time. Doing some reading about it, and attending marriage enrichment events that foster it, are very helpful in making it grow. It is actually possible for two people to be open and honest with each other, to entrust each other with nothing less than the gift of the whole self, and to become increasingly one instead of increasingly two. It takes courage, but it is one of the most satisfying experiences that life offers.

## EXERCISES

1. Take turns expressing your feelings about a particular matter in your life, e.g., your job, a recent exchange you had with each other, your body, the way you relax together, or anything else. You might both choose the same matter, or different ones. The speaker should concentrate on *feelings.* The listener should concentrate on: (a) listening without interrupting, (b) saying back the communication to check it out, and (c) only then responding. After both have done this, share your feelings about communicating with each other in this way.

2. Look back over the eleven suggestions for improving your communication. Each of you pick out two of them you yourself would especially like to work on.

3. If you are somewhat unaware of your feelings, try the practice this week of asking yourself at odd times during the day: What am I feeling right now? Don't give up until you can name it.

4. If you usually say what you *think* about things, practice this week telling your mate at least several times how you *feel* about these same things. For example: When you are angry with me, I feel ... When we make love, I feel ... When I see you with the baby, I feel ... When we are together socially with other people, I feel ...

# 3

# *Dealing with Differences*

JIM AND SALLY MET during their final year at a private college in upstate New York, and married a year later. Jim had grown up in a small town in Connecticut. He was an only child, and his parents were divorced when he was eleven. In college he majored in music, hoping someday to play in a symphony or teach at a university. Jim was quiet and shy, but warm and friendly once people got to know him. Sally had come to the east coast from Montana where her family owned a large cattle ranch. She was the oldest of six children. Sally loved sports and the outdoors, and her energetic, bubbly personality enabled her to make friends easily.

Sally was attracted to Jim's serious, quiet nature. She also liked the order and discipline of his life. Her own family life, relaxed and informal as it was, had at times been confusing and chaotic. Though classical music was foreign to Sally, while they were dating she sometimes bought tickets for a symphony and was fascinated by Jim's knowledge of this

world, so unfamiliar to her. Sally's lively outgoing ways
stirred new life in Jim. He found himself, shortly after meeting her, changing his usual sleeping habits to rise at 5:30
a.m. for a brisk hike, or braving the dampness and cold for a
camping trip. Sally and Jim knew they were different. But
these differences promised to be exciting and enriching. Or
so it seemed during the exhilarating days of their first love.

Sally and Jim were surprised to find themselves viewing
these differences in a new light during the first weeks and
months after their marriage. Differences which had previously delighted them now created problems. Sally became
restless when Jim wanted to spend quiet evenings at home
listening to symphonies or reading about Beethoven and
Bach. Jim no longer wanted to join Sally for hikes and camping. He needed the time, he said, to move ahead in his career. And they discovered other differences. Sally liked a big
sit-down breakfast to start the day, and had many things to
talk about. Jim preferred a cup of coffee to sip while reading
the morning paper. Jim felt uneasy if they were unable to get
to a concert or play early. He disliked starting out at 8:00 for
a performance which began at 8:30. In Sally's relaxed family
climate, no one ever got to an event before the action was
ready to begin. The only thing she worried about was getting a parking place. These differences soon led to irritation
and frequent arguing. Jim and Sally gradually realized that
they had dissimilar ideas about how much time and energy
they would give to making love, making money, worship-
ing God, and other aspects of their life together. Both began
to wonder if perhaps they had married strangers.

However, Jim and Sally's experience is a common one.
We are all individuals with different needs, interests, and
biological rhythms. We squeeze the toothpaste from the top,
middle, or bottom; we sleep with the window open or

closed, with one blanket or two; we like spaghetti and pizza or prefer baked potatoes and ham.

During dating or engagement these differences may not pose a serious problem. Each of us is trying to be as attractive as possible to the other, and we sometimes act a special role. I seem to love baseball; you praise my chocolate cake, although you've never really liked dessert. In the circumstances of dating and courtship we reveal only a part of our behavior or personality to each other. The enthusiasm of romantic love may cause us to conceal or ignore disagreements.

With marriage, circumstances change. We stop acting a special role. We relax and settle in. And there are countless decisions to be made and problems to solve together. Our differences emerge and lead to conflict.

What do we do when conflict arises? This is one of the most critical issues facing couples in the first years of marriage. How we handle conflict is the key to moving from romantic to committed love. Most of the patterns we will use for dealing with our differences as a couple will be shaped during the first years of our marriage. If we make this transition from romantic to committed love our differences can continue to enhance our relationship.

Before reviewing some practical tips for dealing with differences, it is important to examine our basic attitude toward conflict itself. We marry with hopes for a happy life together, and we've learned to think of happiness in terms of peace, joy, warmth, and harmony. When conflicts arise, then, we fear our marriage is a bad one, or that it is in danger. Conflict may trigger memories of our parents' marriages or those of friends and relatives where quarreling and arguments were the order of the day. We had promised ourselves that this would not happen in our own marriage. Yet here we are, faced with conflicts and rising frustration and anger.

Conflict does not mean that our marriage is a mistake or a failure. It is inevitable in any marriage. Differences arise in all close personal relationships. Although we usually regard differences and conflict as a negative experience, they need not be. When we deal effectively with the differences as they arise, we can increase our understanding of each other, love each other more generously, and create a deeper bond. It is when we submerge and ignore differences or use power to bring our mate around to our way that differences are most likely to destroy our marriage.

With this attitude in mind, we will now look at some practical suggestions for talking about differences, resolving conflict, and handling anger.

## TALKING ABOUT DIFFERENCES

1. **Ask your partner to discuss a difference.** When Pam began to resent Walter's behavior in leaving the kitchen a mess, she asked him if they could set aside some time to talk about it. They agreed that they would spend the time after supper the next evening on this issue. It is important to decide when, and sometimes even where and how long, you will talk, and to state the difference you want to discuss. Initiating the discussion at bedtime, or when your mate is busy with something else, or when one or both of you are angry, is not a good idea.

2. **Take one issue at a time.** A key rule in handling conflict is: one issue at a time. Dennis and Chris are discussing the amount of money they spend eating out. He says, "I'm afraid we will never have enough money saved to buy a house if we keep spending this much money on restuarants." Chris replies, "You never really want to spend any time with me. You're always happier when you can have your buddies

over to watch football on TV." With this, Dennis and Chris are off and running. A good fight is shaping up, and they don't even know what it is about. They could argue about whether Dennis loves her, whether he has a right to watch football on TV, or whether his buddies are welcome in the house. They have lost sight of the issue Dennis asked to talk about—saving money—and will make little progress until they can refocus. As any discussion progresses, side roads keep offering themselves for investigation. If we want to make progress, we have to proceed on past them all. We can return to them later.

3. **Stay in the present.** The past can be rehashed endlessly, but it cannot be changed now. We can shape the present and future. Arlene asks Mike if they can talk about the tension that is building over his mother's interference in the way they run their house. Mike replies, "You've never liked my mother, and last Thanksgiving when we were there for dinner, you went out of your way to show your dislike." Now they are looking backward instead of forward. It is usually impossible even to say what really happened in a past event, and, in a conflict, the parties invariably disagree on what happened. Mike could further the discussion much more by exploring the present concern: Arlene's feelings about his mother's interference in their relationship.

4. **Avoid the "Right/Wrong Game"; present your views as opinions and preferences.** We often label differences as superior or inferior ways of being or seeing things. And we usually consider our own way to be superior to our partner's. It is only when we recognize that my culture and your culture are each legitimate but not absolute ways of viewing and dealing with reality that we can move toward the negotiation of our differences. Dave and Nora have different styles of entertaining. He says, "I prefer a simple in-

formal meal, since guests aren't coming primarily for food anyway, and simple meals are easier." Nora responds, "I've always believed that we show guests how much we care about them by our efforts to prepare a really good meal." If Dave and Nora can discuss this difference without labeling one way right and the other wrong, one intelligent and the other stupid, they will learn new things about one another and move toward a resolution of the difficulty.

5. **Talk about the concrete rather than the general or the abstract.** Statements expressed in abstract and general terms are very hard to deal with, and often leave us feeling defensive and confused. Irene says to Tom, "You're always trying to control me." Tom may resent being described that way. Or he may not know how to change it, even though he wants to. What Irene needs to do is spell out for Tom specific situations in which she has felt that way, and the concrete behaviors on Tom's part that resulted in that feeling. For example, "I have to go to you everytime I want money for anything." Likewise, a general comment like, "You never seem to care about me anymore," would be better stated as a specific request, "I need the cards and flowers you used to send to let me know you love me."

6. **Identify the real issue.** When attempts to discuss a conflict run into unusual resistance, it is one clue that there are deeper causes of the conflict than the issue being discussed. Paul and Gina have difficulty settling their conflicts over finances. Each time a decision to spend any sum of money comes up for discussion, they find themselves locked in disagreement. Finally they ask themselves if it is really finances they are in conflict about, and agree to share the deeper feelings and concerns that cluster around this issue

for each of them. Paul admits that he is worried about his ability to succeed in his job and concerned that he might suddenly be laid off. This makes him anxious about spending money. Gina says that she resents the fact that Paul has control of so many areas of their relationship. It makes her feel incompetent and powerless. She has decided that finances is one area she will not let him control. By their willingness to explore the deeper roots of their difference Paul and Gina have learned some important things about one another and their relationship.

7. **Specify where you agree.** The emergence of conflict can put both partners on the defensive, intent on protecting their own position. Therefore, in discussing a difference it helps to find something each of you can agree with in the other's side of the disagreement. Kim and Ray are trying to decide where they will go for their vacation. Kim wants to backpack in the wilderness; Ray prefers a trip to a large city where there are good bars and restaurants. On the surface and in light of their insistence on their own preference, it looks as though they will never come together. But suppose they begin to state their areas of agreement. They find that they both want to stay fairly close to home, that they want time together without others, that neither wants to have to cook on the vacation, and that they'd both like time for reading. Often the areas of agreement are much larger than either partner can see when they are emphasizing their differences. When agreement is highlighted, both persons feel valued and encouraged.

Talking about our differences is the first stage in dealing with them. It helps us understand the issues involved and gives us a chance to listen to each other's needs and feelings. However, even after good sharing and listening, our differences often remain. How do we resolve the conflict?

## RESOLVING THE CONFLICT

We can resolve a conflict in three basic ways: (1) One of us gives in to the other. (2) We agree on a compromise which gives both of us at least something of what we wanted. (3) We agree to disagree and accept each other's right to be different.

1. **One of us gives in to the other.** Although this is the simplest way to resolve a conflict, it is not always easy. Either of us can give the other what he or she wants as a free gift, no strings attached. Perhaps as I look at it I realize that it is not that important to me, that it is a small matter whether we buy this piece of furniture or another, or precisely where the thermostat is set. On the other hand, it may be very important to me, but I may be willing to do it my partner's way as an expression of love. This can be very satisfying and growth-producing for the giver—and for the relationship.

There are two things to keep in mind when resolving a conflict in this way. The first is that a gift is a gift only if it is freely given. It cannot be coerced or demanded. And there should be reciprocity in gift-giving. If one partner does all the giving, that partner soon begins to resent it. This gracious giving of gifts is one of the areas where couples live out the Christian love they promise in the sacrament of marriage.

2. **We agree on a compromise which gives both of us at least something of what we wanted.** Part of arriving at a compromise is exploring the options open to us. Each can then be evaluated for its potential to meet our needs.

This year the vacation will be in the mountains; next year it will be at home.

I'll cook these nights; you cook these.

> I'll go to the baseball game with you this weekend if you
> come with me to a symphony next weekend.

In negotiating a solution to a conflict, each partner has an opportunity to grow, to stretch to see reality from another viewpoint. Each has a chance to show love for the other, and to receive love in return. Each discovers that we have a better chance of getting our own needs met if we try to meet the needs of our partner. There are resemblances between marriage and the ancient tale of the contest between the North Wind and the Sun to get a traveler to remove his coat. The wind tried it first, but the harder he blew, the more tightly the traveler pulled his coat around himself. The sun simply shone, and the traveler removed his coat. That is the way love works.

3. **We agree to disagree.** Sometimes after discussing needs and alternatives we conclude that our differences represent significant value stands and we simply cannot agree. The discussion is closed by accepting each other's right to be different. For example, an area of conflict may be that I approach issues in a calm rational fashion and you get more emotionally involved in them. These may be long-standing personality traits that are not going to change dramatically. In this case we can learn to accept each other as different. Or, I may feel the need for more ritual or prayer in our life; you may not experience such a need. Here again it may be necessary to acknowledge and accept the difference.

All three of these approaches to resolving conflicts depend on the sharing and discussion which has gone on in the preceding stage. In many ways, the *process* of dealing with differences is more important than the outcome. If there is openness and good will, and a real desire to be sensitive to each other's needs, dealing with conflict brings greater closeness.

## HANDLING ANGER

Before we even begin talking about a difference, we may find feelings of anger rising within us. This makes it harder to bring up the topic or to listen when our partner talks about it. How can we deal with our anger so that it does not destroy the possibility of resolving a conflict? There is no simple recipe for coping with anger. A few basic points can help, however.

1. **Feelings are neither good nor bad; they just are.** Anger arises in me. I become aware of it, and I do not want it, but it is there. It is important to realize that feelings are neither good nor bad in themselves; they just are. To feel jealousy, anger, sexual desire, fear, dislike, resentment, or hurt belongs to being human; I cannot escape the onset of these feelings. I am in no way guilty for having them. I *can* decide what I am going to do with them, and for *that* I am responsible. I can choose not to act out my anger. I can choose to go against my fear. But the main point is that anger, even in a close relationship, is one of those things that simply happen. It does not cancel out love. It is not something that "should not be."

2. **Anger usually comes from hurt, frustration, or fear.** When I lash out angrily at someone, there is usually another feeling below the anger—hurt, frustration, or fear. Beneath the anger when my partner flirts with someone at a party and leaves me standing by myself is the hurt I feel at being ignored and seeing another preferred. But it is more difficult to say, "I am hurt," than it is to shout in anger. Shouting, however, works against the marriage. Those who bear the angry attack see only the harsh side of their partners and feel repelled. What we need much more is to know the tender insides of our partners and how vulnerable they are,

so that we become more careful with our power to hurt. But our knowledge is contingent on the honest confession, "I am hurt."

Frustration is another feeling which often lies beneath anger. Frustration is the feeling which arises when I want some good thing and am blocked from getting it. A wife may rail continually at her husband because he will not share more of his feelings with her. She is frustrated in her desire for closeness. Unfortunately, the more she shouts at him, the less he can bring himself to the risk of self-disclosure.

Anger sometimes covers fear. You start asking me questions about something and I get angry because I fear exposure. You put your arm around me and I pull away angrily because I fear closeness or I fear being used. You are surprised when you see my anger. How can I get angry when you put your arm around me? I have to explain to you about my fear.

3. **Reporting anger is much less destructive to a relationship than acting it out.** I can act out or express anger by shouting, and possibly even striking physically. I can act it out by going silent in the relationship. I can act it out by leaving, slamming the door behind me. None of these work well in marriage, where I live day to day in a close relationship with another person. The best way to deal with anger is to report it and to state its cause. "I am angry with you because you are late." This kind of reporting is much easier if we as a couple have come to agree that anger is normal, that it is all right, and that we would much prefer to be told when it is there and what is causing it than to have our partner acting it out in other ways.

4. **A cooling-off period might mean the difference between the destructive and the constructive expression of anger.** Sometimes anger arises suddenly and without

warning, and very strongly, particularly in certain tempera-
ments. The feeling is just too strong to permit any helpful
communication. Then it is better to call time out and walk it
off for a while before bringing the issue back. Cooling down
and reflecting on the whole situation alone, maybe even for a
day, could put matters in an entirely different perspective.
Even after I have told my partner about my feelings, it may
still take time for the anger to go away. I may need some
healing time. I may need to sit for a while, and even pray,
before I can forgive.

It is important to realize that we have some power over
our anger. We can fan it or cool it. We can make and keep
ourselves angry by all kinds of self-talk, rehearsing the incident over and over, and interpreting the other's actions in
the worst possible way. We can recall past offenses too, and
add them on. This fans the anger. Or we can philosophize
about it. "It wasn't that big a deal." "These things happen."
"He didn't mean that much by it." We can elect to lay the
matter aside and move on to other thoughts. We can remember the person's past loving actions. This cools the anger.

Handling anger is important for all aspects of dealing
with differences, from talking about the difference to finding
ways to resolve a conflict. We said at the beginning that differences are inevitable in marriage. It should be clear now
that they are also an opportunity. Married intimacy comes
when we share not only our positive feelings of love and joy,
but also our negative feelings of anger, hurt and frustration,
and work them through. We grow together when we are
aware not only of how we are alike, but of all the ways in
which we are different, and how those differences add interest, vitality, and richness to our relationship.

## EXERCISES

1. Name all the ways you can think of in which you are different. Then explore the ways these differences function to enrich your life together.

2. Take an issue which is a source of conflict in your relationship right now, and try to resolve it in light of the suggestions set forth in this chapter. Begin with a smaller, more manageable conflict so that you can see how the process works, and which suggestions you need to work on most.

3. Discuss how each of your parents dealt with anger, and how you think you have been influenced by them.

4. Review the ways you deal with anger in your relationship. If it has been a problem, discuss how you might deal with it more constructively. Do you:

    (a) feel ashamed of it, and try to hide it?
    (b) give vent to it in violent outbursts?
    (c) keep the hurt, frustration, or fear underneath the anger to yourself, and just give your partner the benefit of the anger?
    (d) act it out by silence, withdrawal, or punishing behavior?
    (e) "gunnysack" grievances until they build up to an explosion over some trivial thing?
    (f) fail to give both of you the benefit of a cooling-off period when anger is very strong?

Choose one way you want to work to change your way of dealing with anger, and share your decision with your partner.

# 4

# *Intimacy and Autonomy*

EIGHT MONTHS AFTER HE MARRIED EVELYN, Tim wrote in his journal:

> I want to be close to Evelyn. But sometimes I wonder, how close is too close? I want to share some really deep parts of myself, but then I get scared and draw back. What if she laughs, uses it against me, or, worse yet, what if I hand over all those things of myself and she leaves me? It's hard to know sometimes how much I want to risk.

> Something else has been bothering me. I just realized yesterday that I haven't taken a walk alone in the woods since we were married. I guess I don't know how I'd explain to Evelyn that I just want to be alone there for a few hours. I think she'd want to come, because she wants us to do everything together, and I don't like to hurt her

feelings. It's just that those times by myself used to be so important to me, and I miss them. Marriage is great, but some parts of it are still a big puzzle to me. Like, how can you get really close to someone and still be yourself?

Tim's question is one that puzzles many married couples. Recently we were at a wedding where the couple shared some of their concerns with the relatives and friends who had gathered there to celebrate with them. They asked their friends to stand by them and help them as they embarked on married life, and said that one of the things they didn't completely understand yet was how their two "I's" could become a "We." Many couples have not formulated the question that clearly. But they experience the struggle. How do we retain our own identities, yet achieve union with one another?

The word "intimate" means getting very close to people, literally "being inside" them. When we think of being intimate, we imagine sharing the inmost part of ourselves, what is most private and personal. Sometimes the word "intimacy" is used simply to mean a sexual relationship, but true intimacy includes much more than that. It is knowing and being known by those I love. I really let them inside, and they let me in. They influence who I am, and I, in turn, influence them. It is the closeness of facing problems and pain, standing together through the major and minor tragedies of life. It is the closeness of sharing significant meanings and feelings, as well as common tasks like maintaining a house, raising a family, or earning a living. It is a closeness born of simply being together without the need to talk, playing volleyball, taking a walk, sharing a sunset.

Intimacy is, in many ways, the key challenge and the deepest joy of marriage. It is the challenge of sharing our life and our world with another. But we can only unite in this way if we are two separate individuals, since only then do we have a self to bring to the new reality that is created in our union. Part of the tension of marriage is this pull between intimacy and autonomy, closeness and individuality.

Much as we long for intimacy, we often find ourselves pulling back and limiting our chances of developing it. Coming close to another gives rise, especially during the first years of marriage, to a number of questions within us: Who am I? Can I take the risk of sharing myself with you? Will you smother me? Can I accept what you will reveal to me about myself? Can I receive your gift of self? Will I still have a space of my own? Am I willing to change? What can I do when we seem to be drifting apart?

## Who Am I?

Closeness with another calls for confidence in who I am. I may find intimacy difficult because I am not aware of my needs, feelings, talents and values. In other words, I do not know myself. The Lutheran pastor Dietrich Bonhoeffer who was hanged by the Nazis during World War II wrote a poem in his prison cell called "Who Am I?" In it he asks: "Am I then really all that which other men tell of? Or am I only what I know of myself, restless and longing and sick, like a bird in a cage? . . . Who am I? They mock me, these lonely questions of mine" (*Letters and Papers From Prison,* p. 348).

Sometimes we find ourselves sharing Bonhoeffer's questions. We want to share our feelings, but we're not certain what we feel. As one wife said, "I don't know yet what I can do. I feel as though I'm just getting in touch with my gifts. So it's hard to bring them out into the open. I'm afraid this new sense I have of them will be lost if I do." Self-disclosure depends on a sense of a self. But our "I" may still be developing and changing. In fact it will be all of our lives. The important thing is to let our partner in on the questions, the struggles, the discoveries of the journey. The gift we give another is always an imperfect and developing self. Even *trying* to reveal it furthers the adventure of discovering it.

## Can I Risk Sharing Myself with You?

In a recent marriage enrichment workshop, we asked the couples for feedback after one of the exercises. One man said, "Before I start to share with my wife, I feel terribly uncomfortable, and I don't want to do it at all. Afterward, the greatest feeling comes over me, and I'm so glad I did." When we attempt intimacy with another, we are risking injury and loss. Exposing ourselves to another makes us vulnerable. What if I share myself with you and you don't like me? If I tell you what I really think about something, will you find me stupid, sentimental, or naive? If I cry and am weak with you, will you use that against me? Are my sexual feelings and fears really O.K., and will you think so if I tell you? All these questions remind us that loving is a risk.

Faced with this risk, some couples pull back. They hide their wounds and pain from one another. They keep even their goals and joys, their experiences of beauty and meaning, to themselves. They may vaguely sense that they aren't as close as they'd like to be, but they don't know why. Bridging this distance requires an act of trust. When I fear the risk of sharing myself with you, I have a chance to express my love for you by moving beyond the fear. I can begin by letting you in on my fear itself. Or I can let you know that I'd like to share more of myself, and ask your help with it. This self-disclosure is a way of "laying down my life for you." As

Jesus showed us, such giving of our life is always costly. He also told us it was the test of true friendship. In addition, it is one of the most satisfying experiences of life.


## Will You Smother Me?

A friend of ours who is considering marriage recently said to us, "My greatest fear is that I will lose my independence. Pete is such a strong personality, I'm afraid he'll just take over and there'll be nothing left of me." Part of her growing sense that she and Pete are ready for marriage is that they are finding ways to deal with these issues of dependence and independence in their relationship. This development of a balance between dependence and independence is one aspect of intimacy.

We said that intimacy can exist only between two persons who remain individuals. In the adjustments and compromises of the first years of marriage we are testing out this tension between autonomy and union to find our comfort zone. If I always accept your view of things, choose the things that interest you most, and let your decisions control our actions, I soon begin to feel that you are swallowing me up. Or, I may be trying to become what I think you want me to be, without even being aware of it. The goal is rather mutual influence. You influence me, and I influence you, and neither of us is destroyed.

Teilhard de Chardin's thoughts on true union can help us. True unity, he says, differentiates. By this he means that center-to-center love should free and foster what is most deeply personal and unique in each of us. Union is a center-to-center loving. It does not blur and confuse what is distinctive about us. It renews and reinforces it. When two dancers are perfectly in harmony, the individuality of each is enhanced.

This insight was very important to one woman who came to talk to us. She had been married nearly ten years, and most of that time she had lived her own life in the shadow of her husband's. She had never finished college herself, and gave little thought to her own gifts and interests. Now she wanted to go back to school and realized that she had real talent in art. But there was a nagging fear that held her back. Would she destroy her marriage if she developed herself? The insight that her artistic abilities, if developed, could actually bring new joy and beauty to her marriage freed her to pursue her studies. She decided to go back to school, and to her husband's and her delight, she deepened her personal gifts and enriched the marriage.

This kind of center-to-center loving doesn't just happen. It depends on a mutual give and take. We must be ready not only to share our ideas and gifts, but to receive and affirm the gifts of our partner.

## Can I Receive Your Gift of Self?

Sometimes we think of love mostly in terms of giving. I show that I love you by doing things for you, by complimenting you, by sharing my feelings with you. That is a part of love. But receiving is also a way of loving, and a very important one. It is love just to listen to your mates, without interrupting, and let them know you really heard what they had to say. It is love to notice how they fixed up the house, or cooked a fine meal, or prepared a surprise gift, to receive it graciously, and to thank them for it. Sometimes it is the respect you give to their ideas and ways that lets them know they are loved and cherished. In one of her love poems, "The Touch," Anne Sexton says that we are all lonely for "something to touch that touches back." Part of this rhythm of touching and touching back in married life is the ability graciously to receive and reverence the gifts, the self, and the influence of our partner.


## Can I Hear What You Reveal to Me About Myself?

I may fear coming close to you because of what I will learn about myself in the process. Sometimes what is hard to take in the first years of marriage is not what we find out about our partner, but what we find out about ourselves. As one young woman who had been married about a year said, "I always thought of myself as a patient and forgiving person. Then I began to wonder if that was just because I had never before gotten close to anyone. In marriage, when John and I began to relate closely, especially in dealing with differences, I saw how small and unforgiving I could be. I discovered a hardness in me I had never experienced before."

This new knowledge of ourselves does not depend on our partner's telling us things outright. That may happen, but the very process of revealing ourselves to another leads to new self-understandings. One woman realized that she had trouble sharing herself sexually because she had such a poor body image. She disliked her body, and the thought of giving it to another made her more aware of this than she had ever been. But it was this very gift of her body to another that enabled her to see and appreciate its beauty for the first time. Living closely with another may make us more aware that we are disorganized, rigid, anxious. All these revelations are invitations to grow. They are grace, and the challenge to new life.

What closeness to another reveals to me about myself is by no means all negative. When we are feeling the pain of learning hard things about ourselves, it is helpful to recall that closeness is also the way we learn that we are lovable, worthwhile, interesting, and valuable persons. Learning these things gives us the courage to face the areas where we still need to grow.

## Am I Willing To Change?

Many people avoid marriage because they are afraid of the ways they might have to change. We cannot come close to another unless we are willing to be transformed by the relationship. There is a well-known passage in Margery Williams' story, *The Velveteen Rabbit,* that illustrates this point. A Skin Horse and a Rabbit have lived side by side in a nursery for some time when the Rabbit asks the Skin Horse one day, "What is Real?" The Skin Horse answers that it happens to you when someone really loves you. He is honest about the fact that it may hurt. He also says, "You become. It takes a long time. That's why it doesn't often happen to people who break easily, or have sharp edges, or who have to be carefully kept" (p. 17). In other words, in an intimate relationship we become, we are transformed. Change always entails both loss and gain.

Usually in the first months of marriage, we realize that we cannot live this closely with someone and refuse to change. I cannot keep coming home from work night after night depressed and refuse to talk about what has happened. I may need to set aside what I would like to do to listen to you at times. I cannot leave the house a mess just because that is the way I have always lived before. "That's just the way I am" is not a very Christian negotiating stance, even if some parts of me are very hard to change. Besides its failure to show love, it deprives me of the satisfactions of developing myself and becoming a genuinely better person. C. S. Lewis puts the matter squarely before our choice.

If you want to make sure of keeping it intact, you must give your heart to no one, not even to an animal. Wrap it carefully round with hobbies and little luxuries; avoid all entanglements; lock it up safe in the casket or coffin of your selfishness. But in that casket—safe, dark, motionless, airless—it will change. It will not be broken; it will become unbreakable, impenetrable, irredeemable (*The Four Loves,* p. 111).

Even when we have chosen to risk change in a relationship, we may face a practical problem. How do I know how much of my independence it is safe to give up? How much can I change and still remain myself?

## Will I Have a Physical and Emotional Space of My Own?

A woman who was recently married said that she found one of the hardest things for her to get used to was having someone else in the same physical space with her all the time. She was not used to having someone else in the same bed, and she did not sleep well at night because of it. When she came home from work she had usually spent a quiet hour reading or writing letters before dinner. Now there was someone there, sharing the kitchen and living room. In the morning she had to share the bathroom with someone else. It all seemed strange to her, since even while growing up she had had her own room to which she could retreat to be alone. Recognizing these feelings enabled her and her husband to find ways to provide some of the space she needed.

One of the adjustments of marriage is the sharing of physical and psychological space with another person. No longer can we schedule times together only when they are convenient for both of us. Nor can we withdraw to our own apartment when we have had a disagreement or quarrel. So we need to learn to respect one another's natural rhythm of aloneness and togetherness, the need for privacy and solitude and for one's own thoughts and interests. Sometimes the problem is complicated by the fact that one partner needs more intimacy and the other needs more autonomy. This then becomes one of those areas where compromise is necessary.

A key to keeping intimacy alive is recognizing that it thrives well, in fact better, when there is some emotional and physical separateness. Otherwise intimacy destroys autonomy. Some couples have understood intimacy to mean that they are to share everything and do everything together. Coupleness becomes the ideal, and both feel guilty if they do things alone. Usually this arrangement cannot be lived for long before one of the partners begins to find it unbearable. We know a very good marriage where the husband went through what he described as "a six-month hell" because he was trying to live according to this ideal, denying his deep need for separateness. When the couple realized what was happening, he felt free to ask for time to himself, knowing that his partner understood. In other words, it is legitimate for spouses to have some separate interests, friends, and activities. A couple we know have been married ten years and have two children. As a Christmas present last year each gave the other a day of solitude and made it possible by taking care of the children that day.

Having a space of our own includes the right to our own thoughts. It's all right for a partner when asked "What are you thinking about?" to reply at times, "It's something I don't care to share, at least not right now." What applies to our thoughts applies to letters and personal property as well. Mail addressed to one partner should not be opened by the other, unless there is a specific agreement that this be done.

We feel violated by a spouse who freely goes through our pockets or purse and opens our mail. Usually when we are tempted to invade our mate's appropriate privacy, it is a sign of our own insecurity. That would be a good thing to talk about. We cannot allow another freedom to be unless we learn to trust. I find it hard to let you out of my sight, so I put pressure on you to keep you at home. I don't like to see you with others, yet I don't want to go with you to a concert, a movie, or a game. So I ask you to give up these interests. This causes resentment, and I can feel you pull away more and more. I lose the very thing I was trying so hard to gain.

Intimacy, as we said at the beginning, must respect the personhood of both partners. Each couple must find that balance of togetherness and separateness that enables them to love one another well. It takes some time and testing to find this balance.

## What Can I Do When We Seem To Be Drifting Apart?

Before marriage it often seems as though we can't find enough time to spend together. Studies, job, family, and even sleep seem to absorb time that we would rather give to one another. As we begin to settle into married life, the pattern often shifts. Now we begin to let these other concerns and responsibilities encroach more and more on our sharing. Gradually we feel ourselves drifting apart.

This disconnectedness lies at the other extreme from the first danger we spoke of, that of stifling our partner's development. Several things may lead to our drifting apart. Perhaps we've begun to make our own decisions about matters that should be mutual concerns, and have stopped consulting one another. Or we no longer share our world of experience with each other. Perhaps we each have our own friends and activities now, and these circles become more and more exclusive. There may be little sex, a lack of a sense of responsibility to one another, and carelessness about making time to be together.

Sometimes one partner is served with a notice of divorce and, taken aback by the news, says that he or she had no idea that there was that much wrong with the marriage. Many times the two have begun to live so completely in their own worlds that they who once vowed to share their lives intimately with one another are now strangers living in the same house. This kind of development illustrates how crucial it is to marriage to keep working at intimacy, because autonomy can get out of control too.

We have talked about some of the challenges couples face around the issues of intimacy and autonomy. Although we have concentrated on some of the problems in these areas, brokenness is not the last word. We may find ourselves drifting at times toward too much closeness or too much separateness. But God is with us in our groping. God so creates human relationships that they have the elasticity to endure healthful stresses. When we have stretched too far, we feel the pain and the pinch. If we have the courage to attend to the pain and talk it through, the power of healing is ever present. And so we remain committed with confidence, to bringing our two "I's" together in a union of love where they become a new "We."

## *EXERCISES*

1. Spend some time alone answering these questions, and then share the answers with your spouse.

   What I like most about myself is . . .
   What I dislike most about myself is . . .

The feelings that I have the most difficulty sharing with you are . . .

The feelings that I can share most easily with you are . . .

2. "What I Love and Cherish in You."

This is an exercise in *receiving* love.

a. Take some time to write down on a piece of paper the things you love and cherish in your mate. Look at your mate physically, emotionally, and spiritually. Include both qualities and particular actions.

b. Take your lists and, facing each other and making some physical contact such as holding hands, take turns exhausting your lists, mentioning all the things you love and cherish in each other.

c. While your partner is telling you these things, your role is to listen and receive, not to analyze or question. Remember, this is an exercise in *receiving* love. So drink it in like a sponge soaking up water, or like parched land drinking in rain. Bask in it as in warm sunshine.

d. When both of you have completed your lists, share any feelings you have about the exchange.

3. Share with each other how your parents handled this issue of intimacy and autonomy. How do you want your marriage to be the same or different?

4. Share with your partner your feelings and concerns about the kind of intimacy and autonomy you now have:

a. Are you satisfied with the amount of time you spend together? The amount of sharing you do?

b. In which of these areas do you feel the need for greater relating: sexual, intellectual, recreational, work, service, spiritual?

c. Are you satisfied with your opportunities for separateness? Is there anything you would like to ask your spouse in this regard?

# 5

# *On the Lighter Side*

KIM AND SALLY HAD SPENT a long and stressful day hanging wallpaper in their dining room. They were tired, but relieved to have finished. Then as they were standing back to admire their work, they noticed that they had hung the final strip of wallpaper upside down. They could have done several things: accused one another, sunk down in discouragement, set to work to repair the mistake. Instead, they looked at one another for a moment, and then burst into long and hearty laughter. The laughter united them in their common dilemma, healed some of their weariness, and threw the whole project of wallpapering into perspective again.

Laughter can do some of these same things in a marriage. It binds us together, lightens our burdens, and keeps things in perspective. Someone has said that the shortest distance between two people is a good belly laugh. We have been talking about some of the struggles of the first two years of marriage and ways to deal with them. All of this can make marriage seem like a very serious business. In some ways it is. But there is another side to marriage, one that is equally important to its success. That is the lighter side. Marriage needs humor, celebrations, play and ritual as much as problem-solving techniques. So in laying the foundations for our marriage we should ask not only "Can we solve conflict?" but "Do we laugh together? Do we play together? Do we celebrate the special occasions of life together?"

## Do We Laugh Together?

One of the reasons humor heals us is that it lets us know it is O.K. to be human. When we can laugh at ourselves it is a way of acknowledging that we are limited. All human beings are, but we sometimes forget it. Then we begin to take ourselves very seriously. We have high expectations for all areas of our lives. We want to be all that a good husband or wife can be: warm, loving, supportive, efficient, thoughtful, successful. But we don't realize all these ideal selves. We lock ourselves out of the car on our way to an important meeting. We invite guests for dinner and the dessert flops. Our partner's relatives arrive for a visit and we make several conversational blunders. Can we laugh at ourselves? Can we allow our mate to laugh at us? If we can, we can live with our imperfections, our failure to be all that we would like to be. And we discover that life is not as tragic as we thought.

Humor also unites us, especially when we can laugh *together.* One of the things that divides married couples is a concentration on each other's limitations. You have faults. You are not perfect. I am finding that you are only human. In fact, I am finding that our marriage is not perfect. When we can share this realization and see the humor in our sometimes awkward attempts to build a life together, it can bind us closer together instead of situating us in opposite camps. Shared humor is a sign of shared values. Part of being married for any length of time is being able to remember together all the ridiculous things we've done. Remember the time we forgot to measure the doorway and bought a sofa we had to hoist up over the balcony? Remember the time we quarreled over where we would go for dinner and then realized we were both talking about the same restaurant but thought it had a different name? Remember the time we hunted for perfect Christmas presents for each other and both ended up buying the same record? All these memories remind us that our mistakes are not final, but can be overcome. In fact, they can enrich our union as much as success when they are shared in love.

Laughter and humor provide perspective. It is easy in marriage for small things to get blown completely out of proportion. You can't carry on a conversation with me until you've had your first cup of coffee. I like all the towels in the bathroom hung in a straight row, and you leave them crooked every day. Humor helps us see that these things are not the earth-shaking events they sometimes seem to be. In view of the larger goods that our life together brings us and the more important positive qualities we find in one another, we can live with them.

## Do We Play Together?

In his small classic, *The Little Prince,* Antoine de Saint Exupéry says: "It is the time you have wasted for your rose that makes your rose so important" (p. 87). Couples at all stages of marriage need time for play. We usually make time for this when we are dating and during courtship. But it can disappear as marriage moves on. We have our careers and financial obligations and goals. We may be beginning a family, or there may already be children in the picture. Our conversations begin to focus more and more on problem solving: Where will we get the money for the house payment? How do you want to rearrange the furniture in the bedroom? Did I tell you about all the problems I encountered at work this week? The pressures of time and the concerns of life begin to erase the playful elements in our relationship. We need to bring them back.

One recent Sunday afternoon we called some friends of ours who are just beginning their third year of marriage. They said that they had just come back from taking a walk to see the autumn leaves, with a stop on the way to buy ice cream cones. "It's something we haven't done for a long time," they said, "something we really needed." Play suspends for a time the serious world of adult responsibility. When we play a game of tennis or baseball, for example, we set up a new time frame and new rules. For a while we let go of the schedules and rules which usually mark our days. That is why play often brings us feelings of liberation and peace. Play provides times when we slow down, get into a completely different mood, and begin to enjoy ourselves and one another. This is a vital ingredient in a relationship.

Play also reveals different and delightful sides of our partner, qualities we don't often see in day-to-day living. We have spoken of the importance of communication in marriage. This non-verbal communication or self-revelation is an important part of it. Play liberates the child in us. It brings out more of the wit and fun, the vulnerability and imagination than we otherwise let each other see. For that reason, it is an important part of intimacy. During these more relaxed times together, free of some of life's pressures, we deepen our bond with one another and build resources for dealing with the harder things we face as a couple.

This importance of playfulness in marital interaction itself has been researched by a Massachusetts clinical psychologist, R. William Betcher. Betcher found that intimate play—teasing or exaggerating, using private nicknames, sharing jokes, making faces, or talking to each other in a childish fashion—can help couples keep a balance between too much distance and too much closeness in their marriage. Such play is also a safe way of approaching sensitive issues or of lightening conflicts. It can often accomplish much more, and in a nicer way, than serious confrontation. Some couples have "fun fights" which make light of their conflicts and differences in a spirit of carefree play and good will. Others use play in expressing intimate thoughts and feelings. A middle-aged couple shared with us examples of this kind of play. Sometimes when he is compulsively rearranging things, she tells him one item is still a half-inch out of place. When he sees her in sweaters on a warm day, he asks if she wouldn't be more comfortable with an overcoat. She tells him he's still not supporting her at the level to which she's become accustomed. And when they pass a beautiful woman in the street, he muses: I wonder if I wouldn't be happier with her. These are some of the ways they keep it light.

The capacity to be silly with each other is an index of the level of trust in our marriage. We are not likely to play in an atmosphere that isn't safe. We have to feel at home to let our child out and act the part of the fool. Betcher recalls a couple who for years had called each other the affectionate name of "Bug." The woman recalled that as a child she and her brothers had used the phrase "snug as a bug in a rug" to suggest warmth and coziness. Now the nickname reminded her and her husband of their experience of being "snug as two bugs" in their relationship.

Humor and play can, of course, be misused. If couples use play to avoid serious communication, it may reveal a fear of intimacy and prevent them from dealing with important issues in their marriage. Likewise, if humor is used to embarrass our partner in public or to cause hurt by poking at vulnerable areas, it is clearly not the sort of play we are suggesting.

We sometimes forget that sex is play too. Media emphasis on sexual performance can cause us to view sex as another area of life where we must produce and live up to expectations. But sex is an important time for relaxation and recreation in marriage. There are no special goals that must be reached, even orgasm. It is a time to be comfortable and at home in one another's love, a time of carefree play. Being able to joke with one another about our sex life is also a healthy sign. It eases tensions in that area and reminds us that sex is meant to be a playful, fun exchange.

Many couples, especially those with children, find that they need to *schedule* time to have fun together. One couple we know plans an occasional "day of madness" together. This is a day they do crazy things they've never done before; they deliberately try to break the mold. They may go roller skating or tobogganing, if these are unusual for them. They may visit the zoo or aquarium, fly kites, or buy balloons or crazy hats. Checking into a motel for the weekend, even if it's in the city, is another way to turn off the problem-solving machine. The important thing is the commitment to spending the time just being with one another. That is often all it takes for the child in us to take over.

One final thing some couples discover is that they need to create some new hobbies or interests that both enjoy. This may mean learning to do something that the other partner likes: playing chess, bowling, hiking. It may mean creating a new hobby. One couple took up folk dancing together shortly after they were married and found that it was one of the best things they ever did for their relationship. As the wife said, "We were too busy learning new steps and finding our way around the dance floor to remember our worries and problems and disagreements." It is after all, as Saint Exupéry says, the time you have wasted for your rose that makes your rose so important.

## Do We Celebrate Special Occasions?

Often when widows or widowers who had been married thirty, forty, or fifty years are asked what advice they would give the newly married, they respond in this way: "I'd tell them to treasure the gift they have in one another and the time they have together. You never know how long you'll have, so take the time *now* to celebrate and appreciate it." Patterns that make room for such celebration are established early in a marriage.

When our concern to produce and achieve becomes too strong in us and prevents us from treasuring the present gift we have in one another, it is helpful to recall that God gives us life as a gift and wants us to enjoy it. A story told by Francis J. McGarrigle, S.J. in *My Father's Will* illustrates this well:

Picture a young mother with her children at the seashore on a summer afternoon. While she sits and reads a short way off, her children play at the water's edge, building sand castles. When they are done they come to her and say, "Mother, come and see what we have made!" So she goes with them.

The oldest says, "Mother, look at my castle. It's the biggest, and has three towers and a wall!" And the mother says, "Yes. Very nice, dear." And the next one says, "Mother, look at my castle! It has a moat where the water comes in!" And the mother says, "Yes, dear. Very nice." The youngest points to a motley pile of sand. "Look, Mom!" And the mother says, "Yes, dear. Very nice."

What does that mother want for her children? That they be safe. That they enjoy the sunshine, the fresh air, the summer's day at the beach, and their own gifts. She knows that the tide will come in and wash the sand flat. She knows that this one day in the life of her children will be lost among all the unremembered days of their lives (Milwaukee: Bruce, 1944).

Like the children in this story, we often make much importance of what we do. In effect, we say to God: "Look what I've done! I've made a fortune! I've kept a clean house! I've raised five children!" And what does God want for us? That we be safe. That we enjoy the gifts of life. That we love one another. In marrying our partner we have received one of the greatest gifts God has to give. What God asks of us is that we accept that gift graciously and richly enjoy it.

One way to acknowledge the gift we have received in our partner is to keep alive the celebration of special occasions in our lives. We cannot afford to forget to mark one another's birthdays with special expressions of love. Couples have various ways of nourishing the spirit of celebration and establishing their own traditions for marking special occasions. One couple we know use their wedding anniversary each year to tell again what they love and cherish in each other. They also spend some time that day reviewing the blessings of the year and of their life together and thanking God for these gifts. Another couple decided that even though they spend major holidays like Thanksgiving and Christmas with their families and relatives, they wanted some of their own rituals to link their years together. So they have their own celebrations first. Each year they make Christmas ornaments for their tree which are symbolic of significant events of that year. And together they cook a special meal to share before they decorate the tree.

Along with the celebration of traditional holidays, a

marriage thrives on spontaneous gifts of love. During courtship we often surprised one another with special cards, a
bouquet of fresh flowers, or a gift we had made with our
own hands. Many married couples testify to the importance
of keeping that element of surprise and those spontaneous
gifts of love alive in their marriage. Some leave one another
love notes when they are not expecting it. Others invite their
mate out spontaneously for a movie or meal. They initiate
lovemaking at an unaccustomed time or place. They plan surprise parties or give cards or gifts that simply say, "I appreciate you today." They put their arms around one another, or
take the other's hand sometimes as they walk along. They
spend kisses freely. They compliment often. We all need to
know often and in unexpected ways that we are loved and
appreciated. Such surprises keep us from falling into the
kind of routine that takes the gifts for granted and notices
only the things we must work on to make our marriage better.

All of these are ways of accenting the lighter side. We
do have to work at our marriages. But in and beyond the
pain and conflict that is sometimes there, and the determination to stand by one another even in hard times, there is the
fact that it is fun to be with one another. These indirect and
gentle ways of humor, surprise, and celebration are as important for our growth as are the more serious and weighty ma-
neuvers. After all, God gave us marriage because he wanted
us to know joy in life.

## EXERCISES

1. Make a "Comfort List" for one another. Take two or
   three minutes making a concrete list of things that your
   partner could do for you during the next week that would

speak to you of his or her love. Try to come up with five or six suggestions and be as concrete as possible. Then exchange lists and choose one or two things from your partner's list which you will commit yourself to doing during the next week. Don't tell your partner what your choices are.

2. Recall some of the most fun times you have had together as a couple and share with one another what made them refreshing for you.

3. Check your schedule together to see if you have some regular fun time with one another built into it. If not, schedule some in and plan some ways to spend it.

4. Talk over the ways you use humor and interactional play in your relating. How might you use them more positively and abundantly?

5. Plan one surprise for your mate for the near future.

6. Spend some time together looking at the way you celebrate special occasions. Talk about some traditions and celebrations you would like to make a part of your life together.

# 6

# *Role Relationships*

WHEN JAN AND CARL MARRIED, each had ideas about what makes a good husband and a good wife. Most of these came from their parents' marriages and those of friends they knew. Jan's father was the breadwinner in the family. He worked long hours as an aerospace engineer, and Jan and her brothers and sisters had been told from the time they were very small that Daddy needed a place of peace and quiet when he came home at night. Jan's mother had nearly finished college when she married, but the demands of being housewife and mother had kept her from returning to school to complete her degree. Jan remembered her mother as the one who cooked the meals, did the cleaning, laundry and shopping, and was there to listen when they fell off a bike, made new friends, or won a part in the school play.

In Carl's home, money was always scarce, and his mother had gone to work when he was four to help support them. Carl remembered the empty house when he came home from school, and the long wait for his mother's arrival and supper. He was determined that his children would not have such an experience. He wanted to succeed well enough in his career as an architect that Jan would not have to work outside the home when they had children.

Besides their own parents, Jan and Carl have other, sometimes conflicting, models of husband and wife. Sam, an architect friend of Carl, is married to a biochemistry professor at the university. Their careers are important to both Sam and Marleen, and they have to work to find time in their demanding schedules to spend together. Two years ago Sam gave up his job with a New York firm to move to Michigan where Marleen had been offered a university position which meant a big career jump for her. Eventually he was also able to secure a job at the university. "We agreed when we were married," says Sam, "that if a real opportunity came for one of us, the other would be willing to move. Marleen would do the same for me."

Jan also has friends who have departed from the images of husband and wife she saw in her own parents. Two of these friends, Mary and Susan, have recently had babies. Both women work outside the home, one as a teacher, the other as a receptionist in a law firm. Mary and Susan worked up to the time their babies were born and returned to work a few months after giving birth. Susan hires a woman to come to their home to care for the baby. Mary's husband, Joe, is a caretaker for a large school with sprawling country grounds. Joe sometimes takes the baby with him while he works, and enjoys his new role of parent to his young daughter. As Susan said to Jan, "Sometimes I feel guilty about hiring someone to do our housework and care for my baby during the day. But I need to continue teaching in order to feel happy and intellectually alive. I just couldn't stay home all day and do housework, much as I love our child."

As Jan and Carl attempt to answer for themselves the question "What does it mean for us to be husband and wife?" they have a variety of models to choose from. At one time it was easier for couples starting married life to know what was expected of them. Culture defined the roles in fairly uniform and clear ways. The husband was the head of the household. The wife cared for the home and family. The husband led in sex and the wife was there to meet his needs. Her husband and children were her main concern, and she was the center of comfort and support for them. The husband managed the finances and the wife furnished affection. He was the stronger, more reasonable force; she was weaker and more emotional.

Men and women are different, the argument ran, and these differences mean that men are dominant and women submissive. In marriage, the wife's identity was derived from her husband's. Fairy tales from our childhood days reinforced these images of man and woman. In these stories of Sleeping Beauty, Cinderella, and Snow White, women wait and receive. Men ride out to slay dragons or battle giants.

As Jan and Carl start their married life, they find themselves questioning these traditional models. For one thing, they have seen them lived out in destructive ways. Take Pete and Sally. Pete has recently been laid off from his job, but he still does not cook or care for their children since he does not see this as a man's task. His wife Sally must do this along with working to support them. Or Mark and Elizabeth. Mark thinks it is his role to manage the checkbook because his dad always did. Actually Elizabeth knows more about math and finances and is much better at it.

Furthermore, Jan and Carl doubt that the old models fit their experience. They are still learning to know themselves and each other, but they wonder: Might Carl be more sensitive to kids, more tender, more of a nurturer? Might Jan be a better financial manager, even a better wage-earner? Might Carl have a better sense of beauty, of detail? Might Jan have a stronger sex need and interest? The conventional images also trouble them because they limit what a husband and wife can hope for from their life together. Jan and Carl want their relationship to foster new discoveries in each other, to free the talents and interests of each, and to leave room for future growth. For all these reasons they are uncomfortable with simply taking over the traditional roles. They need help, however, with some of the questions they face in finding their own way to be faithful and loving husband and wife.

Many couples face these same questions. As they work out their answers, they are providing helpful clues for the rest of us. We want to share some of these insights with you. Since marriage is a journey which lasts a lifetime, you can expect to adjust these roles many times during the course of your life together. However, a good beginning will make much difference in the way the journey goes.

## HIERARCHY OR MUTUALITY? THE CHOICE IS YOURS

1. **Hierarchy: Dominance and Submission.** You can think of your relationship as husband and wife in two different ways. One we will call hierarchy. Although this term can be used in a variety of ways, we are using it here to describe unequal parties. Picture a pyramid with someone at the top in control of those at the bottom. Or a ladder, with someone ahead and someone behind. Since two parties in a hierarchical relationship are not considered equal, one has more power and dominates. Although there have been some matriarchal societies, cultures generally have put the man rather than the woman on top in marriage. This model has meant

that it is the wife's duty to allow her identity and life ambition to be absorbed into those of her husband. If decisions are to be made about careers, it is the wife who gives up her career goals. In this model the husband is expected to be more active, rational, and strong. The wife, by contrast, is more passive, emotional, and dependent.

We have often turned to the Bible to support this traditional relationship between male and female, husband and wife. The story of Adam and Eve is a familiar example. Arguments from the order of their creation, Adam first and Eve second, find their way into many discussions of the role of male and female. Basing their opinions on these Genesis accounts, some early Christian writers argued that only man was created in the image of God. Woman shared in that image only through man. Countless writers throughout the centuries have used the Hebrew Scriptures to defend woman's subordinate position and to determine her role in the marriage relationship. Many New Testament passages are also used as part of this argument. For example, Ephesians 5:22–33, where a wife is exhorted to be subject in everything to her husband and show him all respect, has frequently been read at weddings.

Hierarchy has long been the dominant model in marriage relationships. Many married couples have found that it worked well for them and it still appeals to many today. Couples choosing this model generally have a clear idea of what it means to be husband and wife, since the roles are quite well defined. However, in recent history many women have begun to struggle against their subordinate and inferior position. Men have also begun to see that though their position appeared to have more power, it meant carrying a heavy burden and denying whole parts of their personality. As one man said, "It's no wonder I have trouble talking about my feelings in our marriage. It was never O.K. in our house for a man to have feelings, let alone cry in public. I couldn't even cry when my little brother got hit by a car." Meanwhile, women no longer believe that loving their husbands well demands that they deny their own ambitions and energies. They believe that their gifts and goals are just as important as their husbands'. Roles in a marriage need not be based primarily on gender differences.

Couples who find that the hierarchy model does not suit their marriage relationship are developing new patterns for relating to one another. One pattern that appeals to many is based on the notion of mutuality. It is probably evident from this whole book that this is where our sympathies lie, as it seems to give more scope to the full Christian personhood of both husband and wife.

2. **Mutuality: Free To Relate as Whole Persons.** Mutuality means tumbling the pyramid so that husband and wife are no longer relating from a position of power and powerlessness. Rather, they meet as two whole persons who respect and love each other as equals. A husband and wife striving for mutuality in their relationship will each at times be emotional or rational, weak or strong, active or passive. At times he may initiate sex; at other times she will. Sometimes he will feel insecure and needy, turning to her for support; at other times she will be weak and vulnerable.

Mutuality is the exchange of gifts between persons who do not wish to establish their own importance at the expense of another's gifts. As husband and wife we put our individual gifts at the service of our common relationship. We are ready to recognize qualities of tenderness, initiative, or compassion, whether they occur in male or female. Then in the rhythm of our life together we can affirm these gifts. We do not label them superior or inferior.

Couples who are attracted to the model of mutuality

may wonder what biblical basis there is for this approach. How deal with readings from Genesis or St. Paul?

Reading the Genesis accounts today, Scripture scholars can see that it was not the writer's intention to place woman in a subordinate position. In fact, there is a growing consensus among scholars that a relationship of dominance and inequality between man and woman enters the world only through sin. Both male and female are created in God's image, and together they constitute humanity in its fullness. Woman is not man's "helpmate," but a companion equal to him. This theme is repeated in another book of the Bible, the Song of Songs. Set in a garden, the book depicts paradise recovered, and celebrates human love. It is a mutual love, in which both man and woman give and receive, initiate and follow, delighting in one another's beauty. This love, they declare, is "strong as death. . . . No flood can quench it" (8:6–7).

When St. Paul makes statements placing women in subordinate positions, he is often simply calling on social and cultural customs of his time to settle disputes and restore order in the churches. He is not describing an ideal for Christian relationships. And there is another side to Paul. He is aware that commitment to Christ demands a new pattern of male/female relationships. Holding up such a vision to the Christians in Galatia, he quotes part of an early baptismal formula to show what kind of relationships should exist among those who have joined the Christian community.

> All baptized in Christ, you have all clothed yourselves in Christ, and there are no more distinctions between Jew and Greek, slave and free, male and female, but all of you are one in Christ Jesus (*Gal 3:27–28*).

The Christian vision calls for a change in cultural patterns. Those who belong to Christ are equal. They are not to set up categories of superiority, dominance and control. So, marriage in Christ must reflect this new pattern of relationships between man and woman. It requires mutual respect and recognition of gifts.

This may seem too exalted an ideal when we look at our day-to-day attempts to live with each other. None of us is yet a whole person. We bring to our marriage many questions about our personal identity, and perhaps especially our sexual identity. Our career choice may just be emerging, and it may change several times over the course of our married life. Yet, within a relationship of mutuality these gifts can gradually emerge and be nurtured in each of us as they do, free from the blocks set up by convention or fear. Trust and acceptance allow us to explore and understand dimensions of our self we have never looked at before. We can acknowledge our own gentleness, strength, assertiveness, or fear, and share these qualities with our partner and receive our partner's gift in return.

## FINDING YOUR WAY: SOME PRACTICAL GUIDELINES

Three practical suggestions may help you as you begin to answer for yourselves the question, "What does it mean for us to be husband and wife?" They are: (1) Don't make assumptions about areas of responsibility; make joint decisions. (2) Let your talents and interests be your guide. (3) Resist pressure from family and friends.

1. **Don't make assumptions about areas of responsibility; make joint decisions.** One potential battleground during the first years of marriage is household chores. *Who* will do *what* in maintaining our common life? Who makes out the budget and pays the bills? Who cooks when we en-

tertain? Who cleans the bathroom and does the laundry? Who sees that there is food in the house? Who washes the dishes and when? Who mows the lawn? And, if there are children, who takes care of the children?

As we move into marriage we may believe that if we really love each other these things will take care of themselves, that love will conquer all. It seems unromantic and unnecessary to sit down and plan such details. You might have to do this kind of thing when you are living with a roommate, you reason, but not with a spouse.

Unfortunately, it is not that automatic in marriage either. When neither person has agreed to make the coffee and it is too late to get it ready, both partners start the day in a bad mood. Guests arrive and the house is a mess. He says, "Why can't you keep this place looking decent?" She replies, "I thought you'd be taking care of that for a change." Lots of energy is used up dealing again and again with details like who will go shopping on this day or who will pay the bills this week. Lack of planning produces confusion and unpleasant scenes. He decides to stop on the way home from work to do the shopping. Instead of receiving praise, he is greeted with a frown and, "I already got bread and fruit." If it is *assumed* that one partner is chief cook and bottle washer, that partner may resent this assumption.

Do not leave these matters to chance, traditional assumptions, or daily discussion. Sit down and make some decisions together.

2. **In deciding what roles each will play, look to your talents and interests as a primary indicator.** One problem many couples have with traditional role descriptions is that they ignore skill and choice. A husband may be expected to be the handyman fixing things around the house when in fact he is not handy at all. A wife may think she

should be the principal cook even though the only cookbook in which she has ever felt any interest is the *I Hate To Cook Book*.

Some couples find it helpful to list the regular responsibilities demanded by their life together. Then they decide who is best suited to handle each. These tasks need not be limited to areas already well developed. Perhaps you have always wanted to bake bread, but have been afraid to try. If I am patient with your efforts, you have a chance to develop a new talent. Likewise, I may never before have been in charge of the maintenance of a car or learned to change a tire. I will feel increasingly independent and competent if I am allowed to take over that area and learn about it. However we first apportion the tasks, it is important to keep dialoguing and adjusting accordingly, since interests and needs keep changing.

Sometimes neither of us will want to take care of a particular task. This is another one of those times when we learn what love is in day-to-day life. One description of love tells us that we love someone when we care as much about that person's welfare and happiness as we do about our own. A good way to show this is by offering to shop when we don't want to be bothered, or by doing the cooking when both of us are very busy. It is here that Christian virtues like consideration and self-giving love find their greatest scope in a marriage.

3. **Resist pressure from family and friends.** Bob much prefers to stay home and work. He likes to shop and cook and care for their child. His deepest desire has always been to become a good poet, and he finds that he has some time left each day to work on his poetry. His wife Julie has long wanted a career as a fashion buyer. She finds the competition and pressure of the job exhilarating, and she loves

the contacts she makes through her job. She is happy to carry the responsibility for financial support of the family. Bob and Julie's chief problem comes from dealing with family and friends.

Bob's parents often say to him, "We thought we raised you to be a man. Now you can't even hold down a regular job. Writing poetry and taking care of kids is fine, but it's women's work. Where did we fail?" Friends ask Julie, "How can you neglect your home and family for a career? How can your child get the love he needs when you spend so little time with him?" On the other hand, couples who opt for traditional roles because this choice suits them best have to deal with similar comments. How many women in this situation have been asked "Do you work?" or "How can you stand just being at home all day?"

A couple's own communication and comfort level with their choices is the most important ingredient in handling comments from family and friends. Once we are deeply convinced and in agreement about how to be husband and wife to one another, it is easier to explain our choices to others—or not to explain them. At times we may choose to use humor or to ignore these questions.

With these practical tips we end our discussion of one challenge of the first two years of marriage: working out for ourselves what it means to be husband and wife. We have seen that when the conventional answers to this question do not satisfy our own hopes as individuals and as a married couple, we may be left on our own with few clear models to turn to. And we may meet objections and pressure from family and friends when we begin to work out our own models. But the weakening of traditional cultural norms can also be a positive event for our marriage. It can free us from the fears that would prevent our independently determining areas of responsibility and sharing. This process of finding our way is not always simple and seldom without pain. Each model we work out has some positive aspects and entails some loss. But the new flexibility does help us to undertake a journey with surprising and enriching turns and discoveries.

## *EXERCISES*

1. Reflect on the marriages you have known, especially that of your parents. What kind of role relationships did they have? How have these marriages influenced your own idea of what it means to be a husband or wife?

2. Tell one another about any feelings of confusion or any conflicting movements you find within yourself as you think about what it means to be a good wife or husband.

3. Look together at the way you have divided up your household tasks. Does this sharing of responsibilities best express the talents and interests of both of you? In what ways would you like the sharing to be different?

4. What things have you always wanted to do that you were afraid to try because they did not fit with the male/female stereotypes you had been taught?

# 7

# *Sex*

DON THOUGHT everything pointed to a good sexual relationship with Sue when they got married. The sexual expression they permitted themselves during their courtship had been exciting and satisfying and had left them feeling very close to one another. Sue had held back a little, it was true, but Don figured once they were married and had their own place, their sexual expression would be very free, fully mutual, and frequent. It would bring years of masturbating to an end for him.

Sue's sexual upbringing had been very strict, and deep-down she felt less than comfortable with the whole matter. In her family, sex was never spoken of, and the implicit message was that it was a shameful thing. Her church reinforced the impression. Her sex education was scanty at best, and her experience very limited. She loved the physical closeness with Don, but felt considerably less sure about anything genital. Her hope was that once they were married, her inhibitions would go away and everything would work out.

The trouble began on the honeymoon. Don was ready to go, and could not understand Sue's reluctance at all. After all, this was what marriage was really all about, wasn't it? Sue in turn discovered that the marriage ceremony did not make everything come right, but that she continued to feel awkward, unsure, and a little ashamed.

As the months went on, Don became increasingly impatient, as the dashing of his hopes was a bitter disappointment. His impatience and anger came across to Sue as a demand, and she began to see him as interested in one thing only, with no respect for her feelings. The more of that she saw, the more she pulled back.

It took Don and Sue a year and a half to work out their sexual relationship, and there was much pain along the way. The first and hardest thing they had to learn was that they needed to open up to one another and talk about it. It wasn't just going to take care of itself. Then there were discoveries. The main one was that they were very different people sexually, and had to work out compromises in this area as in every other. Both had to work on their attitudes. Don had to develop sensitivity. He had to learn important things about the whole context in which lovemaking occurs or does not occur. Sue had to overcome her childhood conditioning and acquire a more positive view of this whole aspect of human life.

Don and Sue's experience has its own particularities, but almost every couple has to work out difficulties in their sexual relationship. It is liberating to realize that. Developing a mutually satisfying sexual relationship takes time, a lot of communication, and considerable experimenting. The first two years are crucial in laying the foundations. There will be discovery, as both persons come to know their own bodies and sexual emotions under many different circumstances. At the same time, they will be getting to know each other sexually. There will be integration, as sexuality finds its place in the larger context of the total relationship, including the couple's Christian faith.

Let us examine some of the myths about sex which create problems for people. Then let us itemize some of the ingredients of a satisfying sexual relationship. Finally, let us see what light our Christian faith sheds on our experience of sex.

Our treatment focuses on the relational aspect of sex rather than on the procreative. The procreative is surely a basic and wonderful dimension of it, and we treat "The First Child" in Chapter 9. We focus here on the relational aspect because many couples have more trouble relating to one another sexually than they do bringing children into the world.

## Some Myths About Sex

1. **Sex is a performance.** It is an area of life in which you must come off looking good. Pleasing a woman sexually proves your manhood. Pleasing a man sexually proves your womanhood. Sex is serious business. There should be no talking, no laughter, and no hesitations. The goal and test of success is orgasm for both parties. After it's over, you can light up a cigarette. Mission accomplished.

Such is the myth. The only trouble is, a performance always brings performance anxiety. What if I don't have an orgasm? Should I fake it? What if I have erection problems? Or have trouble lasting long enough to bring her to orgasm? What if the techniques the book described don't work on this person? The greater the anxiety, the greater the possibility of failure. Trying to have an orgasm is like trying to make yourself fall asleep. And coming to sex afraid that you might have erection problems is like coming to a conversation afraid that you might stutter. The feared thing happens, precisely because you are thinking about it so much. Wouldn't it be a relief if we could define sex in some other way than as a performance?

Yes. Actually, sex is communication. It is a way of telling someone of your love. You can be a little bit clumsy about it, and still get the message across. Sex is play. It is a way two people who love one another relax together and give each other refreshment. Orgasm may occur in the process, but it is not the goal. Because sex is communication and sex is play, there might well be some conversation mixed in with it, and some humor as well.

2. **Sex is the responsibility of the man.** The man is the aggressor, after all. The woman is supposed to be passive. The woman has little interest in sex anyway; she could take it or leave it. But the man is always ready and looking for his chance. The woman waits—or avoids.

This is an injustice to both sexes. Women enjoy sex as much as men do, if the sexual encounter takes place the way they like it. In many couples, the woman has more sexual interest than the man. It is a burden for the man to carry all the responsibility. He begins to feel oversexed, unloved, or both. Often he feels like a beggar.

In a good sexual relationship, either the man or the woman might initiate more often. Or they might initiate about equally. There is no rule about this, except that the sexual relationship should not be all one person's responsibility. Also, in a good sexual relationship, either partner has the right to turn down the offer when not in the mood.

3. **All physical contact must lead to sex.** After all, would a man or woman have any other reason to touch one another?

Yes, fortunately they do. Touch is an expression of caring, of comforting, of expressing warm affection. Someone once said that everybody needs four hugs a day for survival, eight for adequate functioning, and twelve for growth. When a woman says to her husband: "The only time you ever touch me is when you want sex," she points to a real problem. She feels used, not loved. And she will probably pull back from any gestures of physical affection because she knows exactly where they are going. This leaves the relationship poor indeed.

To many people, it is a great value just to be held. It gives more comfort and security than sex. To others, a backrub or massage is a most welcome gift, saying all the same things that sex does. A marital relationship is greatly nourished by frequent embracing. This is a good thing for the kids to see too—and to experience themselves.

4. **Sex equals intercourse.** What else is it? There is foreplay, which is a preparation for intercourse, which ends with orgasm.

The problem with this myth is that it so clearly defines the sexual encounter that it establishes a routine which can easily become boring, and it imposes some real pressure both to perform and to enjoy it whether you like it or not. Many turn away from all sexual approaches because they do not like this rigid sequence. Others are blocked by it from discovering what it is they really enjoy sexually.

The great therapist, Milton Erikson, in dealing with couples who had sexual problems, compared having sex to having an elaborate meal. There are several courses, each to be enjoyed for its own goodness. You don't rush through the soup to get to the salad. Nor do you start with the main course. You might pause a while before bringing on dessert, just to talk. Or you might skip dessert altogether, because the meal has been quite satisfying without it. You take some care in preparing an elaborate dinner. You don't do it every day. The occasion has to be right. You attend carefully to the details—the tablecloth, the candles, the lighting, the music, your attire and appearance. You might start with some hors d'oeuvres. Probably you will still be at the table talking for some time after the meal is over.

When a couple is taken through sex therapy, the first rule enjoined on them is that they should not have intercourse. They should also not strive to have an orgasm. If it happens, O.K. Instead, they should go back to the beginnings of physical pleasuring—embraces, kissing, petting, fondling—to rediscover the things that give them pleasure and bring feelings of closeness. This greatly lessens performance anxiety, and enables many couples to discover what they really enjoy sexually. Often enough, it is not intercourse. A couple may fondle each other genitally before going to sleep, or on awakening in the morning, without any intention of having intercourse.

5. A couple's sexual relationship falls naturally into place. We are sexual beings by nature. The desire is strong and the mechanics are easy. When two people are attracted to each other, their sexual relating will probably be one of the easiest aspects of their life together.

Would that it were this easy. No, the myth offers a false promise, and so makes matters worse. Establishing a good sexual relationship takes the same kind of work that putting the rest of married life on good foundations does. Individuals vary greatly in their sexuality—in their degree of interest, in what pleases them, in the circumstances that are important for enjoyable sex. Because of the differences, and because of the difficulty many couples find in talking about sex very openly, coming to sexual comfortableness with each other does take time. We need to give each other permission to "go slowly," to be awkward, to try things without fear, to ask for help, to make mistakes, to get to know ourselves and each other gradually over time.

Having considered some of the myths, and the truths they misrepresent, let us focus on a few more of the factors that make for a good sexual relationship.

### Four Essentials

1. **Information.** This is the sort of thing we wish our parents or some school had given us, but they haven't always. Fortunately, it is easy to acquire these days in the form of several popular books, some of which are listed at the end of this book. Being basically informed about male and female anatomy and function, male and female sexual response, and the kinds of things that many men and women enjoy puts us in a better position to adjust well to this aspect of our relationship.

2. **Communication.** Developing a good sexual relationship depends vitally on good communication. We can read a number of books on how to make love to a woman, but only this woman can tell us how to make love to her. We can fantasize fantastic sex, but if we want its execution, we have to tell our mate what our fantasy is. In a good sexual relationship, we do not just go along forever with whatever our mate is doing. We tell each other what we like and what we do not like, and we ask for what we want. Each of us feels free to turn down sexual overtures, usually stating why.

What we are describing here is not so easy to achieve. In

the sexual encounter, all of us are vulnerable. It can be very scary to talk about it much. It can be hard to ask for what we want, and risky to try something new. What we need to do is create a space in which both of us are safe. What we have said about viewing sex as communication and as play should be helpful here. Some other suggestions may help too.

We know a couple who do journaling about what they have especially enjoyed sexually, and share their journals with each other as a prelude to talking about it further. They find they can be more frank this way than they usually are if they just start talking. Now they have begun to write their sexual fantasies down—the way they would really like it to be—and are sharing these with each other.

Another couple uses "show and tell" communication to help each other understand what each likes. They show each other where they like to be touched and how, as they talk about it. Or they take each other's hand and guide it according to what they like.

Reading books together and discussing them is another way to get communication going. Reading breaks the ice and serves as a springboard for personal exchanges. One way to put some new things into practice is to take turns trying them. This week, you lead the way, decide on the place and time, set the stage, take the initiative, and ask for whatever you want. I will follow. Next week, I take the lead. After each experience, we do some debriefing, sharing our feelings.

3. Love. Good sexual technique is marvelous, but the great turn-on is still love. Our sexual response is very closely tied to whether we feel loved and cared for or not. Part of this is helping each other feel good about our bodies; many people need assurance that their bodies are beautiful to their partners. Part of it is accepting each other where we are in

the whole sexual adventure, and being patient and encouraging. And part of it is learning to *receive* the gift of love. One of the best ways we can give sexual satisfaction to our partners is to let them experience us responding with pleasure to what they are doing.

4. **Context.** Sex lives in a context, and depends vitally on the context for its meaningfulness and development. It is a kind of barometer of how the relationship as a whole is going. Good sex needs good feelings about each other. When sex is going badly, look for stored-up feelings of anger. It is very difficult to make love with someone you are angry at. It goes best in the dark, and usually does not take very long. Most people simply avoid it. Probably the worst situation is when the anger comes right into the sexual relationship and is expressed there, in insults about the other's body or sexual adequacy. Sex lives in a context. It is the open, playful, relaxed, and joyous celebration of a love that is going on all the time. It re-expresses that love, and in so doing strengthens it, and leads away again into further practical expressions of it.

Kevin and Marlene came in for counseling three or four months after their first child was born. Their relationship was on the rocks, but each expressed quite different concerns. Her complaint was that he never helped around the house, cooked a meal, did the dishes, or took the child off her hands. What was worrying him was that after the birth of the child, she seemed to lose all interest in sex. She did not initiate anymore, and refused him more frequently. When they had sex, she seldom had orgasm, which had never been a problem before. He wondered if perhaps she had suffered some physical damage in childbirth.

The therapist quickly put two and two together and acted on a hunch. He took Kevin aside and told him that he thought the key to recovering his sexual relationship was doing some housework. Kevin was dubious, but agreed to go home and tell Marlene that from that night on he would take care of the dishes. He started changing the baby and cleaning the house once in a while. Two weeks later, it was a rather different couple who visited the marriage counselor. Marlene was surprised how much more responsible Kevin had become, and related incidents of his helpfulness. Kevin told how Marlene was showing her old interest in lovemaking, and had recovered her responsiveness. A rather simple change had taken place. For three or four months, Marlene had not felt loved. Now she did again. When people feel loved, they feel like loving.

## Sex in the Context of Christian Faith

We opened this chapter with the story of a person whose religious formation became a block in her married sexual relationship. Unfortunately, such persons are not rare. Religion and sex have not always been friends. In its treatment of sexuality, religion has usually devoted most of its energy to trying to prevent the evils which irresponsible sex breeds. This is useful, but it is certainly partial. The side of sexuality which religion so often neglects is its character as gift and revelation, a thing to be wondered at, enjoyed, and celebrated in the Lord. Our concern here is not with promiscuity but with sex in the context of married love. What does Christian faith have to say to that? Does it merely concede that the use of sex in marriage is unobjectionable, or does it have other light to shed?

All creation is the revelation of God. In other words, all things that are made show forth something of the mystery of God. Indeed, all created things contain God and bear God to us as gift, a gift inviting response, a gift inviting relationship.

We sit before sunsets in wonder. We experience God beside quiet lakes, in deep forests, before majestic mountains. We marvel at the faces of children, at the movement of gymnasts and dancers, at the musical expression of the great composers. Some people say they experience God in childbirth. Others ask: Who could see a rose and doubt God's existence? But flowers are the sex organs of plants. And does no one experience God in the act of making love with another human being? Where is wonder greater than here—or the goodness of living more profoundly experienced?

The human body is a beautiful thing. Painters, sculptors, and photographers have labored through the centuries to capture and celebrate its glory. On the streets of the city, all of us have turned our heads more than once in pursuit of its passing. It is the image of God that arrests our attention. For Genesis tells us that it is in God's own image that we are created, male and female. The New Testament adds another dimension: "Do you not know that your body is a temple of the Holy Spirit, which you have from God?" (1 Cor 6:19). The body is a sacred place, where God dwells and is manifested. The body's beauty and mystery are prominent in the sexual expression and celebration of love. God is there.

But the relationship between God and human sexuality runs deeper still. God is love. We experience the mystery of God whenever love touches our lives. The love of God has countless embodiments, but the best of them are human persons who love us. The person who has covenanted love to us for life and lives it in myriad details, who stands by us in good times and in bad, who knows all about us and loves us anyway, that person is a very special incarnation of God's love for us. The experience of married love, sexually expressed, is the experience of God's own tenderness. For God *is* love.

So we know and believe the love God has for us. God is love, and the person who abides in love abides in God and God in that person ( *1 Jn 4:16* ).

Beloved, let us love one another; for love is of God, and the person who loves is born of God and knows God. Anyone who does not love does not know God, for God is love ( *1 Jn 4:7–8* ).

When human beings make love, and live it, they abide in God and God in them. When I make love to you, it is God's own love for you that I mediate.

Sex, in other words, is an important part of Christian spirituality. The contemplative vision to which Scripture invites us enables us to see sex not only as one of God's great gifts, but also one of the places where God gives self. Perhaps this is why the mystery of sexuality has such power and affects us so profoundly. In Christian marriage, reflection on sexuality ought to shift from fear of possible wrongdoing to an open embrace of the religious experience God wishes to give.

## *EXERCISES*

1. Take a few moments to recall one or two of the best sexual experiences you have had with your mate. Share with each other what was special about the experiences.

2. Share with each other what you like about your present sexual relationship. Be as specific as you can.

3. What change would you like to ask of your mate where your sexual relationship is concerned?

4. What factors, if any, do you see inhibiting your sexual relationship—e.g., anger, performance anxiety, childhood messages about sexuality, early sexual experiences, poor body image, lack of communication about what you enjoy and do not enjoy? What can you do to overcome these difficulties?

5. Take a few minutes for each of you to write out a sexual fantasy you have had involving your mate. Share these. Then plan the times for each of you to lead the way in bringing the fantasy to life.

6. Select a book you will read together and discuss.

7. Share with your mate how you view married sexuality in the perspective of your faith.

# 8

# *Families and Friends*

MARK AND KAREN HAVE BEEN MARRIED about a year. At least every other weekend, Karen drives a hundred miles to be with her parents. Mark goes along about half the time. When he does, he spends most of the weekend watching TV with Karen's brother, while Karen talks with one or both of her parents about various things or goes out with her mother. Karen is very close to her mother, and spent three weeks with her when her mother had minor surgery. She is also "Daddy's little girl." When Karen has a problem, she goes to talk it over with her parents. They helped her decide on a job change. They have also advised her from time to time on how to deal with Mark. Mark does not have a job, though he works part-time at various things and usually takes a course each semester at a nearby community college. Mark has erection problems. This was a painful discovery for both of them. They have dealt with it by putting it on the shelf. With very rare exceptions, they simply avoid sexual intimacy.

Karen and Mark are not really married, though they went through an official public wedding ceremony a year ago. Karen, as you can see, has never really left home. And Mark does not seem to mind too much. He is not ready for the responsibilities of marriage either. His erection problems accurately reflect his position in his relationship with Karen, and in the world at large, and that is probably where they are rooted.

The Book of Genesis, right after it tells us that God created us male and female, says: "This is why a man leaves his father and mother and joins himself to his wife, and they become one body" (Gen 2:24). The passage makes it clear that marriage entails a weighty decision. By it, two persons establish a new community, which becomes primary for them, and all their other relationships change in the light of it. The individual is no longer alone, but has a life companion now, and must be aware of the impact of all choices and behaviors on him or her. Important decisions are joint now, no longer unilateral. So when Paul says to Susan, "Oh, by the way, honey, my folks are coming up the weekend of the 27th," he has forgotten that he is married, and Susan feels it at once.

It is quite different with Mike and Jo. Jo came from a very closely knit family, and when Mike came into her life, the family was not too sure he was the right man for her. Mike felt that lack of welcome every time he was with Jo's family, and he knew as the relationship became serious that pressure was being put on Jo to break it off. They went ahead with it anyway, even though Jo's parents threatened to boycott the wedding, and nearly did. A few weeks after the wedding, as interference continued, Mike told Jo she had a choice to make. It was either him or her family. He wanted nothing more to do with them. With a heavy heart, Jo chose Mike, and the two of them moved to another city. They have a six-month old baby now, and Jo's parents have never seen her. There are no visits, no letters, no calls, by Mike's rules. Jo cheats only occasionally, making a collect call when Mike is gone, or slipping a snapshot into the mail. She feels guilty when she does it. She does not like the way her family has dealt with Mike, but she loves and keenly misses her family. She also wonders what effect it will have on their children to be deprived of one set of grandparents, aunts, and uncles. She and Mike do not talk about it. It is one of those forbidden subjects.

Jo and Mike show us the opposite extreme. It is called cut-off, and cut-off is a good name for it because it is a little bit like trying to cut off your arm. You are dealing with something vital, and there are unmistakable effects. Jo's family is still present in Mike and Jo's home, present like ghosts in the empty chairs. They are also present in Mike and Jo's struggles with one another, even if they are never named. What Jo and Mike have not been able to work out with Jo's family, they will continue to try to work out, perhaps without knowing it, in other internal and external conflicts. They would do much better to return to the original problem, and try again to solve it. Cut-off is not a solution.

When two people come together in marriage, each emerges from a long-standing network of family and friends. As they work out their relationships with all these people, now as a married couple, they have to keep two truths in mind. The first is that marriage is a new community of a very significant sort, in which two persons become in some sense one, and their relationship to each other takes precedence over every other. The other truth is that each party to the marriage marries not just an individual but in some sense a whole community, and they will continue to need those communities. Put another way, you marry just one person, but you marry into an extended family. The business of retaining all these prior relationships, or at least most of them, while also changing all of them in light of the new reality, is no small challenge. It is a crucial part of laying the foundations for a good marriage in the first two years. Let us look first at the challenges of relating to family, then the challenges of relating to friends.

## Relating to Family

Problems with in-laws are not at all uncommon in marriages, and often the struggle continues well beyond the first two years. Sometimes parents do not want their child to marry at all, because of the loss involved. Sometimes they disapprove of their child's choice. Sometimes they have quite definite ideas about jobs, finances, housekeeping, and the proper parenting of their grandchildren, and they continue to assert these ideas even in a marriage they approve of. And sometimes they are just needy, and want a lot of time. Not seldom, they are powerful people and show great determination.

The cardinal principle in dealing with in-laws is that united we stand, divided we fall. In that respect, it is much like dealing with children. If an in-law can do a wide end-run around one of the partners, or slip quietly between them because there is plenty of space, the game is up. If the husband passively watches TV while his wife is taught good housekeeping and proper parenting by his mother, he is effectively on his parents' side, and his wife is one against three. A united couple is a far more formidable force. The couple's unity is precisely what shows the in-laws that their relationships to their child have changed, that a new reality exists, and that a boundary line has been drawn. What this implies is that a couple has figured out together what they want their relationships to in-laws to be, how much time they want to spend with them, and how much suggestion or gentle pressure they are open to before they reassert the boundary.

Good relationships with one's own parents in adult life demand that one has "individuated" from them or become one's own person. I have to do this as an adult whether I marry or not. It means that I am comfortable both agreeing and disagreeing with my parents, pleasing them and disappointing them. I am not governed by their preferences for the shape of my life, even though I give those preferences a respectful hearing. And I do not submit to the idea that I exist to make my parents happy. No, they have to make their own happiness, as everyone does. I like to contribute to it, but I have to be my own person and live my own life. I respect my parents, but I demand that they respect me too. I am an adult. I leave my parents free, and I require that they leave me free as well.

This is a major growth step, and it takes time. It usually begins in teenage rebellion, and comes to completion in subsequent years. It can be more difficult when the relationship is good than when it is not. One of the scary parts of it is that when I have individuated from my parents, I have to make it on my own. That is what Karen, at the beginning of this chapter, was not ready to do. And her parents did not want to let go of her either, so they had a great thing going—at the expense of her marriage and her maturity. If one has not individuated from parents, one is not going to make a united stand with one's mate so that the two can expand in a new stage of growth.

Joan and Jim live just a few miles from Joan's parents. The parents have no more children left at home and their marriage is not a very happy one. Joan and Jim's marriage is going pretty well, so the folks come over about three times a week, at least once for dinner. Joan has a hard time putting up with her mother's endless stream of suggestions on how to keep a house and kitchen clean, and how to deal with a baby. After her mother leaves, Joan finds herself seething within, and she vents to Jim, who agrees that her mother is pretty hard to take. Joan's father brings his own brand of dogmatism to the situation, and all listen without interrupting, including Joan's mother, though admittedly attention is not perfect. Joan's ideas on the relative importance of a spic-and-span house and a perfectly disciplined child differ from her mother's, but with her mother coming so frequently she does not get much chance to try them. Joan hates to rock the boat. She was raised with the idea that parents are to be respected and obeyed, no questions asked. Jim stays out of it. He figures this is a problem between Joan and her family. He also happens to dislike confrontation.

There are several problems involved here. One is Joan's difficulty in individuating. Another is the lack of a united front. A third is the unexamined assumption that Joan and Jim are in the service of her parents' happiness. A fourth is their common unwillingness to be assertive about what they are feeling. The result is that the parents have all the power in the situation.

In-law relationships are delicate. Most of us love our parents. Whatever their shortcomings, they have given us a lot. And usually we are important to them, and they want very much to continue to give to us and to receive. Often they help set us up financially when we are not very strong. They partially furnish our new living space out of their attic. They are happy enough to take care of our children. Their counsel is often invaluable, as they have fought their way through so many challenges before us. Their own needs for affection and appreciation continue after we have left home.

The extended family is a great human resource. They offer us models, both positive and negative. Meeting our mate's parents and brothers and sisters is a great help in understanding our mate more fully. The love and moral support of all these people is important to us and to our children through the years.

If cut-off is disastrous, not only for the victims but also for the victimizers, the art is to work out ways of getting on together. That, of course, is the basic art of marriage itself, and it demands some compromise here as there. While Joan and Jim are not in the service of their parents' happiness, they do care about it, and so will be willing to spend more time with them than they might really want to. They will try to be patient with what they find irritating, and let some things go. But they will also be firm in their insistence on certain things.

From a Christian perspective, what we are trying to manage here is the difficult business of loving where many differing interests are involved. We owe it to our spouses to be good to their families. And as spouses we owe it to one another to be sensitive to each other's feelings and needs. As children, we owe respect and love to our parents. Weighing all these factors, we try to make the best decisions we can about how often to have our parents over, where to spend the holidays or vacation, and generally how much time we have to give to our families of origin and how much we need to be by ourselves or with others. We need not be too surprised if our parents are not perfectly satisfied with our choices. Most people have to win their freedom from their parents, wresting it away in a kind of struggle. Parents do not usually give it as a free gift, because they feel the loss so keenly. Someday we will probably have to go through this ourselves. It is usually up to the children to set the new boundaries.

Where relationships remain strained, many people find it more workable to keep visits brief and make them more frequent, rather than have long ones. Trouble usually occurs some time into the visit, after the news has been exchanged and the enjoyable things done together. Then the excitement wears off and patience and prudence begin to grow thin. It is best to be on the road by this time, with a promise to return.


## Relating to Friends

Betty was a little surprised in the first months of her marriage when Bob's friends would suddenly appear on evenings and weekends and invite him out for racquetball. Nodding to her, they would engage Bob in conversation and before very long he would drop what he had been doing and go off with them. "We're going to play some racquetball. See you later, hon," he would say, and the door would close behind them. Sometimes Bob's friends would come, and, with the same nod in Betty's direction, sit down and have a few beers. They were all old friends, and had been doing this sort of thing together for years. "Yes," Betty thought, "but hasn't there been a bit of a change in Bob's life? Where do I fit in, anyway?"

It was quite different with Sue and Lou. Lou did not have many friends when they got married, and felt no great loss in disconnecting with the ones he had. His vision of it was that he and Sue would be enough for one another. They would do everything together. It bothered him a lot that Sue did not drop her old friends in the same way. But Sue had a rather different sort of friendships, deep ones, with two women she had been close to for several years. She liked doing many things with Lou, but noticed that there were some elements in her he could not understand or address, and she still derived deep satisfaction from being with her women friends. It took Sue and Lou most of the first year to work through this tension.

Lou gradually came to realize that he really had nothing

going in his life except Sue, and that he was asking her to be a whole world to him. Even if she had had nothing else to do, she could not have fulfilled this expectation. But there were a few other things Sue wanted out of life as well. Lou started to feel better when he returned to finish school, looking toward a job that would be more satisfying to him. He also took up sports again, an interest Sue did not share, and he developed some new friendships there. His jealousy of Sue's relationships abated as his own world expanded, and as he realized that she could love her friends without loving him less, for love is not a limited quantity.

All living is an act of balancing. It is walking a tightrope with a long pole, pushing it neither too far to the right nor too far to the left. One extreme in the present frame is acting as if two people can fulfill one another entirely, can meet all one another's needs, with no help from God or anybody else. This is imprisoning, stifling, and likely to end in violence when one of the parties can stand it no longer and has to break out. The other extreme is going on living as if one were still single, except that there is another person in the house now to be at one's disposal as the need arises. That person will probably not stay very long.

It is not so easy to work out what is mine, what is thine, and what is ours, but each of these categories has its place in marriage even where friends are concerned. Before our relationship developed, we each had separate friends, some of them very special ones. Is it reasonable to expect that we will want to let go of them? Is it reasonable to expect that you and my long-time friends will become friends with each other in the same degree that they and I are? It does happen occasionally. But more commonly, that special something that two friends have had cannot be fully shared by a new marriage partner. The best way to handle it seems to be to have some threesome time, but to allow for the old twosome time also. Thus the friendship is incorporated into the marriage, but it continues to enjoy a life of its own. The key to allowing this, rather than being jealous of it and trying to kill it, is realizing that every person has legitimate needs that go beyond what the marital relationship can meet. Besides, love exists in us as an abundant quantity. It is not like a budget, where money spent here is no longer available for use there. I can spend time with my friend, and come back with *more,* not less, love to share with you.

What about friends of the opposite sex? This is a higher risk, and often does not work as well. It is harder for one's mate to trust, and well it might be, for it is harder for one to behave with the opposite sex. Everything depends on the strength of the marriage, the maturity of the partners, and the chemistry of the friendship. When these things are in good shape, such relationships can be managed successfully and be a real enrichment, but they do require responsibility and care.

Might an old friend be a married person's primary confidant? When John became depressed in the first year of his marriage, it was to his old friend Andy that he turned, and it was Andy who helped him uncover the root of his troubles. When Sue wants to talk about religion, she goes to her friend Rita, because John has only a basic interest and not much knowledge in that area. Sue has wished it could be otherwise, but it is not, and so she gets most of her religious needs met outside the marriage. This seems like a good use of friends.

It is a different matter when a person outside the marriage becomes the primary confidant and closest friend. For then the question arises: What is the marriage? If the marriage partner is the last to hear the news, if almost all marital conversation is about the practicalities of keeping the household going, if one's psychic energy and social time are more bound up with someone outside the marriage than with one's spouse, the marriage has died or is dying. The present state of things is a far cry from the courtship period, when two hearts beat as one and lovers could hardly wait to be together, when there were no secrets, when the feeling of being understood was complete. Someone has stopped talking. Or perhaps someone has stopped listening.

It is a great help to couples to develop new couple friendships together. Besides the friendships which will form through casual association, there are sometimes groups that form after retreats or marriage enrichment events. Four couples of our acquaintance have taken their own initiative in forming a couple support system. These four couples get together once a month to talk about the struggles they face in relating to one another and to their children. If one of the couples is going through a difficult time together, the group acts as support and also shares experiences that may help the troubled couple deal with their difficulties. Whether it be casual friends or more formal groups, a network of other couples is a vital resource in keeping a marriage strong.

In this whole area of relationships with families and friends, we are looking again at challenges to Christian growth. Can I become large enough to let you go and let you grow in ways that are good for you, even if I am not directly involved? Can I overcome my selfishness and do battle with my insecurity? Can I open my heart wide enough to embrace your family and friends because they are dear to you, even if there are some of them I don't like very much and others that threaten me? If our relationships with parents are strained, are we willing to seek reconciliation and keep trying to work things out? If we feel they are encroaching on our freedom as adults, can we summon up both the courage and the gentleness to tell them the truth with love? If we can answer yes to these things, we are living the vocation and growing with it. Our love will deepen and others too will find life in the circle of its warmth.

## *EXERCISES*

1. Reflect on the following questions for yourself:

   a. Have I really left home?
   b. Do I realize that my parents' happiness is not my re-sponsibility but theirs?
   c. Can I make decisions for my life which do not neces-sarily have my parents' approval?
   d. Am I showing my parents a basic respect, loyalty, and care?

   Ask your mate to evaluate you under the same headings.

2. Share with your mate any difficulties you feel in the way he or she relates to your parents and family.

3. Examine your friendships with people outside the mar-riage. Does each of you, and do both of you together, have enough outside support and stimulation to keep you going and growing? Are these friendships secondary to and compatible with your marriage? Share your thoughts with your mate.

4. What do you think God's call to growth to you is in this area of relationships with family and friends?

# 9

# *The First Child*

DAVE AND KELLY'S FIRST CHILD brought a revolution in their marriage which put a real strain on their relationship. Dave and Kelly had known each other for three years, and married in their mid-twenties. Both of them very much enjoyed the bar scene. They liked to drink, dance, and play pool. Dave had become especially adept at pool, and was making a little money at it. He began to get into tournament play. Dave and Kelly had planned to have children sooner or later, but the pregnancy occurred before they were psychologically ready and took them both back a bit.

As the child grew in her, Kelly herself began to change. She felt she was outgrowing the bar scene. As she felt herself becoming a mother, she wanted to drink less and stay home more. She was no longer in much condition for dancing anyway.

When the child was born, she felt a deep joy, and tended the baby with the greatest affection. As far as Dave was concerned, the birth was all right, no big deal. But it began to bother him increasingly that Kelly so seldom wanted to go out to the bars with him. What he had thought was a special problem belonging to the last months of pregnancy and the first months after childbirth began to establish itself as a pattern. Kelly had simply moved on to another stage of life. In outside relationships too, she began to gravitate toward other young mothers rather than to their former bar friends.

Dave could see it only in competitive terms. The baby had taken over the love which used to be his. Fighting increased. Neither seemed to be able to get through to the other. Dave spent little time with the baby, whom he resented, and considerable time away. Since much of the time they spent together went into the argument they could not resolve, Kelly had little appetite for lovemaking. Matters got worse until Kelly and Dave finally parted.

Not all stories of a first child end this way, of course. A child can bring many blessings to a marriage. But Dave and Kelly's story points to some of the factors which need to be considered before a newly married couple is ready for a child, and some of the adjustments which will be required when the child comes. In this chapter we will look both at the challenges and at the blessings. Let us consider the challenges first.

### The Challenges of Childbearing

1. **Lifestyle.** The adjustment begins early, with the beginning of pregnancy itself. "Your body begins to prepare you," one young mother told us. "Pregnancy starts to cut into your working and social life. You feel like staying home more, which is what you will have to do when the baby comes. You have to watch more carefully what you eat and drink, and that will continue as you breast-feed. You become

uncomfortable during the night, and sometimes the baby's movements awaken you, a preparation for nights to come. Already you are losing some of your freedom, and the summons to think beyond yourself and your mate is already there."

During pregnancy, the life of the father is affected too. His wife is tired, and sick more often. Sometimes she is moody or depressed, as pregnancy brings physiological change. In some ways, she grows more inward, focused on the life developing inside. She usually wants to share with him what she is feeling and thinking about during this period, but it takes some evidence of interest, patience, and understanding on his part. In their absence, she may feel unhappily alone and unappreciated, and possibly even resentful. Sickness, fatigue, and moodiness may bring changes to a couple's lovemaking patterns. The emerging mother may feel less interest, at least in intercourse. On the other hand, she may need and appreciate being held and other signs of affection more than ever. She may also need to be assured that her body is still beautiful, in some ways more beautiful than ever.

2. Finances. The first child makes a financial impact. First there are maternity clothes. Then there are outlays for furniture, clothes, toys, and food for the baby. There are all the medical expenses of pregnancy, childbirth, and followup care. Another expense will become a budget item after the birth—babysitting. Perhaps the greatest impact of all will come from a mother's leaving the workforce near the end of pregnancy and staying out for some months or years to come. If a couple has become accustomed to two incomes, and the woman's identity and life-satisfaction derive heavily from her work outside the home, this will be a major adjustment. "It took me about a year," one mother told us, "to

feel I didn't have to work outside the home. It was hard for me to feel I was still a contributing member of the family. The change also meant we had to do without some things we had previously enjoyed."

3. **Responsibilities.** Some couples do not discuss parental responsibilities very much beforehand, and developments catch them unprepared. The adjustments are challenging enough even with good preparation. For instance, who will do what after the baby is born? Who will get up during the night, if it is not a question of breast-feeding? Who will get up to take care of the baby or young child on weekend mornings? Will Dad ever take care of the child all day Saturday or Sunday (or both) while Mom goes off to other pursuits? If Mom did all the cooking and housecleaning before the child came, will she simply continue to do so after the birth? If so, resentment is likely to build, because taking care of a baby or young child all day every day is extremely demanding. "What galls me," a new mother told us, "is that he still expects his dinner to be on the table every night when he gets home, including weekends, and when dinner is finished he goes out to the living room to watch TV." Another said, "He still loves his job more than anything else. That's supposed to be his domain, and home and kids are supposed to be mine. It would mean so much to me if we could share both areas more."

Sometimes a husband realizes what an impact a new child has had, and genuinely wants to help his wife. But he comes to her as helper, awaiting his assignment, rather than as someone who is really taking responsibility. If asked, he will shop, do the laundry, or clean the house. But he expects to be thanked when he is finished, and then the responsibility is hers again. What is much more helpful to the new mother is when her husband simply takes over the cleaning, or the shopping, or some of the cooking, and makes them his own. Now he is a collaborator rather than a helper. Now they will be thanking *each other* for taking care of various parenting and household tasks. It is interesting how the bones of contention in unhappy marriages are the gifts which husband and wife freely give one another in marriages that work. This gift-giving is contagious, as well as fun.

> Give, and it will be given to you; good measure, pressed down, shaken together, and running over they will pour into your lap. For the measure you use with others they in turn will use with you (*Lk 6:38*).

4. **The couple relationship itself.** The first child brings some loss of freedom to both husband and wife. No longer can they simply get up and go out whenever they want to. The needs of a third person must always be taken into account. When a fourth is added to the third, all moves become still more complex. But it is not just a question of going out. It becomes more difficult to make time for each other. Since fatigue is already one of the major factors affecting a couple's sexual relationship, the fatigue that comes with pregnancy and child care will also have to be figured in. Uninterrupted adult conversation will also be harder to manage. And getting away to be together will now involve the difficulty of finding and the cost of paying a babysitter.

And yet a couple has to be creative in continuing to make time for each other and for the relationship, or all family members will suffer. If they are not careful, they will soon know one another only as parents, no longer as friends and lovers. They will have a price to pay for that someday, even if they can manage to stave off payment until the last child leaves home and they are left staring across the living room at one another as strangers. Much anguish can be avoided if they are aware of the danger and taking measures against it all the time. We make time for the things that seem important to us. Can we afford not to make time to remain friends and lovers? Being good parents is important. But if we allow distance to develop between us, we can hardly even be good parents, let alone models of marriage for our children. In any case, our couple relationship remains primary. It will outlive the parenting function by many years.

Sharing time together as a couple, and sharing the parenting, are the best remedies for a husband's developing jealousy over what happens to his wife as she becomes a mother. Then he does not stand outside that new relationship, but inside of it. He has his own relationship to his child, and still a primary relationship to his wife, whom he also supports in her role as mother. "When I hear a man brag that he has never changed a diaper in his life, it pains me," a young mother told us. "What a loss. There is nothing dirty about changing a diaper. It is a great chance to fondle and tickle and kiss and play with your baby. My husband cherishes the chance as much as I do. And the baby loves it."

In light of the various challenges we have considered, when is a couple ready to have their first child? Some couples do not have the leisure to ask the question. They are pregnant when they marry, or they already have children from a previous marriage. For those who do have the leisure to consider the question, the answer is: when they have looked at all the implications and feel ready—that is, when the financial conditions are in place, the impact on the marriage has been measured and plans made for dealing with the new responsibilities, and, above all, when the marital relationship itself is stable and promising. There are plenty of challenges at the beginning of marriage just in terms of living together as a couple, and it seems like a good idea to weather these before taking on the added responsibility of a child. Couples sometimes hope a child will pull a struggling marriage together. That is a very risky bet. A new presence in the home can hardly solve the problems. It will make many of them more acute. Studies are clear on this. When a marriage is in trouble, it is not a good time to have a child.

## The Blessings

The challenges to a married couple which come from bringing a child into the world are only part of the story. The blessings also abound. Childbearing is the other part of the mystery and gift of sexuality. It is the power and privilege of being able to co-create with God, to cooperate in generating and fashioning a new human being. Much excitement and happiness attend this process when the stage is properly set for it.

. Don and Terri waited longer than many couples do, or need to, before they decided to have a child—four years. Children were in their pre-marriage plans, but career and other considerations counseled delay. In fact, Don and Terri were not that sure of their marriage all through the first three years. Then some breakthroughs occurred in their communication, and a new spirit of concession and cooperation was born. With a fresh confidence in each other and in their ability to make it together for life, they revived their discussion of children and decided it was time.

As they made their plans and began actively to seek conception, Don and Terri noticed a strengthening of the bond between them. For the first time since the days they had planned for their marriage, they felt that they were working together toward the same goal. Then they were greeted with a surprise. Six months went by and there was still no conception. It seemed a very long time to them, and they wondered if it would ever end. It made them doubt their own fertility. As they prayed over it, they came to a deep realization: Life is a gift, and it comes from the hand of God. They could do certain things. But the matter ultimately rested with God. Late in the seventh month conception did occur, and Terri and Don rejoiced exceedingly, the way the people of the Old Testament rejoiced when a couple was blessed with a child.

New realizations came to Terri and Don as the pregnancy developed. There were so *many* things outside their control—the sex of the child, the color of its eyes, the makeup of its personality, even its health. They began to see themselves more as caretakers of a human person who would be entrusted to them than as its owners, and in wonder they lived with the gradual hidden fashioning of the body and spirit of this new person. Terri marveled at the preparation of her own body and emotions for this new stage of her life. Along with the wonder and worship went the usual sickness and fatigue, and Terri and Don were challenged to adjust to these developments.

The process of childbirth and the tiny, perfectly formed body of their new little boy were further cause for amazement. The boy knew how to suck at the breast without ever having been taught, and the mother/child bond was deepened through this experience of feeding. Terri reflected on the religious meaning of the gift of the body—hers to Don and his to her in sexual relating, and now her gift of the body to this little infant as physical presence, warmth, and food. She understood more profoundly the meaning of Christ's gift of the body to us in the Eucharist, the gift of the body being the gift of the self as food and life. Breast-feeding times became for her occasions of this sort of simple contemplation. She found herself quietly marveling at the deep mystery of things.

In the months that followed, Terri and Don watched the

gradual emergence of the personality—the grasping of the little hands, the first hesitant smile, the dawning of curiosity. Then came the crawling, the standing on two uncertain legs, and the first faltering steps. Never having watched this development so closely in anyone else before, Don and Terri were amazed at each stage in the process. There were laughs, and there were truly precious moments to share. As the child's life unfolded, their deepest sense was that a real gift had been given to them, and that one of the most important things they had to do the rest of their life was to love that child.

Another young mother told us how she felt a strong desire to clean the house as the day for delivery drew near. She had all the carpets shampooed and the walls washed, so that the baby would have a really clean environment. And then she awoke on a deeper level still. She felt a movement of the Spirit within to do something about her own house, to clean out the locked up room within herself. She took care of some things she had long put off, and ended with the sacrament of reconciliation. After that, she felt ready, at peace with herself and the world.

One of the things children do is show you yourself in a way you have not seen yourself before. In their interaction with you, they reflect you back to yourself. Much of what you see is beautiful, and you didn't know it was in you. Children give you an opportunity to see sides of each other that you had not seen before. The husband watches in amazement as the mother comes out of the wife. The wife watches in joy as the father comes out of the husband. It is often a pleasure to stand back and watch the interaction between the child and your mate; it makes your mate dearer.

There is another side to this mirroring too. "She made us clean up our act," a young couple said. "We started watching our language. We became more aware of patterns of behavior we did not want to model for her. Why, she even got us back to church. We found ourselves examining our whole way of life in the light of our new responsibility, because we really wanted to do right by this child." And so there is a blessed stretching that takes place as a couple becomes generative. Their time is no longer their own. They have to make sacrifices, as they learn to expand their love to embrace each successive newcomer.

Sometimes God is seen and understood in a new way as a result of the parenting experience. The father of a one-year-old boy told us that his son changed his whole image of God. "I look at that little boy and I see myself in him. Every once in a while he gets a look or makes a gesture that is a perfect reproduction of me. And he is so lovable, you know? What has come home to me is that God sees me that way, and loves me the way I love that little boy." A young mother told us her little girl changed her whole outlook on life. "She wakes up every morning eager to greet the new day, with a smile as big as the sun. She is rarin' to go. How can you get out of bed grumpy with someone like that in the house?"

We talked to a couple of parents of many years, whose children were raised. A woman told us she would not have exchanged the experience for anything. Her children, she said, had taught her most of the really valuable things she knew, had made her the person she was. The other was a father of nine, who had raised his children on a tight salary through many years of hard work and sacrifice. On his deathbed, he was asked by one of his children whether it hadn't been a terribly heavy burden all those years, and whether he hadn't had second thoughts about it all from time to time. "Oh, no," he said with a happy smile. "It was all worth it. It was great fun."

## EXERCISES

1. If you do not have a child but are planning to have your first soon, discuss with each other your hopes and fears in the areas of:

| | |
|---|---|
| timing | parenting the infant |
| finances | your sexual |
| household | relationship |
| responsibilities | individual and |
| job responsibilities | couple freedom |

Think of some things you might do to keep your relationship as a couple growing even as the parenting goes on.

2. If you already have your first child, review together how its coming has affected your marriage. If either of you is experiencing difficulty, discuss how you can change what is happening to make the situation better.

3. If you already have a child or children, discuss the blessings they have brought to your marriage. Where do you catch a glimpse of God in your children? What new beauty or character do you see in your mate, now become father or mother? What changes are you aware of in yourself?

# 10

# *The Spiritual Dimension*

IT WAS A BEAUTIFUL WEDDING. Jamie and Paul had spent a lot of time planning it. They selected their own Scripture readings and wrote their own vows, trying to express something of what they understood Christian marriage to be. But after the celebration was over, Jamie and Paul found it hard to see much of a connection between the church ceremony and their daily attempts to build a married life together. They had wanted their marriage to be built on a strong faith in God, but it was hard to see a relationship between those idealistic statements in Genesis about becoming "two in one flesh" and the struggles they were having over where to hang pictures in their new apartment. Maybe, they reasoned, they would have time for the religious aspects of marriage after they got some of these practical matters out of the way.

Jamie and Paul are not alone in thinking that religion is something added on to married life, an extra activity alongside our efforts to build a good marriage. Many couples think of the religious aspect of their marriage as consisting mainly of church services, prayer times, and other religious activities. The fact is, however, that it is not primarily the church ceremony which makes marriage a sacrament. It is the way a Christian man and woman live their whole life together. They love one another in the spirit of Christ, living Jesus' great commandment especially well. Because of this, the invisible becomes visible in their marriage. The love of God is revealed in their love for one another. Whenever the invisible appears in the visible, you have a sacrament.

There is a Jewish rabbinic story which expresses well this truth that God's love is found in the experience of human love.

Time before time, when the world was young, two brothers shared a field and a mill, each night dividing evenly the grain they had ground together during the day. One brother lived alone; the other had a wife and a large family. Now the single brother thought to himself one day, "It isn't really fair that we divide the grain evenly. I have only myself to care for, but my brother has children to feed." So each night he secretly took some of his grain to his brother's granary to see that he was never without.

But the married brother said to himself one day, "It isn't really fair that we divide the grain evenly, because I have children to provide for me in my old age, but my brother has no one. What will he do when he's old?" So every night he secretly took some of *his* grain to his brother's granary. As a result, both of them always found their supply of grain mysteriously replenished each morning.

Then one night they met each other halfway between their two houses, suddenly realized what had been happening, and embraced each other in love. The story is that God witnessed their meeting and proclaimed, "This is a holy place—a place of love—and here it is that my temple shall be built." And so it was. The holy place, where God is made known to his people, is the place where human beings discover each other in love (Belden C. Lane, "Rabbinical Stories," *Christian Century*, December 16, 1981).

This story says well much of what we want to say about Christian marriage as a sacrament. Both in the marriage ceremony and in the life that unfolds from it, the married couple give each other the sacrament. The gift of the self to one another *is* the sacrament, the place where God appears. As we have shown, the self is given through sharing one's inner feelings and one's body in sexual expression, as well as in all the ways two people serve and help one another. Each reveals God to the other in the way they love, for God is love. Prayer and religious practices are important, but they are meant to support the efforts of the married couple to live out Christ's command: "Love one another as I have loved you." Marriage is a call to love a particular imperfect human being as Christ loves him or her. This vocation involves us in faithfulness, forgiveness, generosity and gift-giving, telling the truth with love, gratitude, dying and rising, and outreach to others. These are the virtues of Christian marriage. Let us look at each of them.

1. **Faithfulness.** In our marriage vows we promise lifelong fidelity to our spouse. This promise of faithfulness means more than just staying with someone, and more than just sexual fidelity. It means working on our own growth: our addictions, our depression, our temper. It is also a commitment to growth as a couple as we discover new things about our spouse and ourselves, and as life keeps presenting us with new challenges.

We discover early that we are different. You are for a

tight budget; I am given to spontaneous spending. You find me a poor companion where your feelings are concerned; I am disappointed because you don't seem to enjoy sex very much. Along with these differences we find that we can hurt each other in many ways. The challenge a couple faces is: Can they love one another? Will he stick with, and work it out with, this particular flesh-and-blood woman, and will she stick with, and work it out with, this particular flesh-and-blood man, both with all their imperfections? That is the Christian challenge.

Along with the call to fidelity, God gives a married couple the help they need to live it out. When a man and woman covenant their faithfulness to one another, God also covenants faithfulness to both of them. God promises, "I will be with you," in the daily struggles and decisions. God's faithfulness gives us the courage to embark on and persist in this tremendous adventure of love.

2. **Forgiveness.** A grace that is especially important to our faithfulness in marriage is the ability to forgive and be forgiven. A marriage can last only if there is a capacity on both sides to forgive. Forgiveness does not come easily. We all have a tendency to hang on to our hurts, and to bring them up again. Forgiveness gives power away; it says: I won't hold you to it, won't use it to bargain, won't look upon it as permission to return you an evil. I may still feel the hurt or injury, but, without denying it, I freely release you from my resentment.

Sometimes married couples are asked to forgive large hurts, perhaps even infidelity. But usually it is the lesser and far more frequent failures of daily life together that require forgiveness—the lapses of memory, the moods, the insensitivities, the stubbornness, the hurting remarks or silences.

Forgiveness is an important value in Jesus' view of the

world. There is his own example, with the one who denied
him (Jn 21), and with those who put him to death (Lk
23:34). There is the parable of the merciless debtor (Mt 18).
Probably even more important for the day-to-day living out
of a marriage is Jesus' answer to Peter's question:

> "Lord, how often must I forgive my brother if he wrongs
> me? As often as seven times?" Jesus answered, "Not sev-
> en, I tell you, but seventy times seven times" (Mt 18:21–
> 22).

Closely related to forgiveness is acceptance. It is forgiveness for the way one is. Sometimes married couples
insist on keeping each other reminded of all their
shortcomings. He keeps reminding her that she is not a great
housekeeper. She keeps him alert to the fact that she doesn't
like his smoking and never did. He lets her know regularly
that she is not too intelligent. She is careful not to let him
forget that he lacks social skills. What is the point of keeping
each other feeling bad about things they feel bad enough
about already? This is not how love acts.

> Love is patient and kind; love is not jealous or boastful; it
> is not arrogant or rude. Love does not insist on its own
> way; it is not irritable or resentful; it does not rejoice at
> wrong, but rejoices in the right. Love bears all things, be-
> lieves all things, hopes all things, endures all things (1
> Cor 13:4–7).

3. **Generosity and Gift-Giving.** The director of a marriage and family therapy program recently remarked that we
are much better today at teaching people how to meet their
own needs than we are at teaching them how to sacrifice,
hang in there, and give to one another. This is another important area for married couples' growth in the Christian

life. As one young man said after being married for six months: "I never knew how selfish I was till I got married."

What we would prefer to do and what love demands will not always coincide. There will be many opportunities for generosity and gift-giving, as we saw in the chapter on dealing with differences. This is one of the ways in which the call to love awaits us in the ordinary moments of our lives. We recently talked with a couple who were each in an armed camp, filled with grievances. She liked movies; he wouldn't go. He liked hunting and fishing; she stayed home. They tried to build a house together, and fought over the design and furnishings of every room. Neither was willing to compromise or give to the other.

There is a Gospel paradox involved in the business of compromise. It is the very heart of the Gospel, in fact: you have to lose your life to find it. This runs against a deep human instinct—to save my life, to protect it, to make it secure. Some married couples take the stance, "I would give, *if* . . ." "I will give, *when* . . ." This is the instinctive attempt to save one's own life and to venture in love only when it is clearly safe. The trouble is, it won't work.

> For anyone who wants to save his life will lose it; but anyone who loses his life for my sake, and for the sake of the Gospel, will save it (*Mk 8:35*).

We do not find life by demanding it as a right. We find it by giving it away in love. Then it comes back as a gift, unexpectedly. The willingness to compromise, to do it entirely your way sometimes and to go halfway to meet you at others, is one of the ways I must give up life to find it.

4. **Telling the Truth with Love.** Yet part of life is assertiveness. Sometimes Christian spirituality sounds as if it is

all give, all concede, all grin and bear it. Is there no room in it for a complaint, for negative feedback, for the expression of pained feelings? There is.

When two people live closely together and want to love each other truly, feelings need to be dealt with openly and honestly, or they will make much mischief beneath a placid surface. We talked about this in our chapter on communication. If you don't feel understood, you had better tell me, and add why. If we have expectations of one another where household tasks are concerned, we had better make them known. Telling the truth with love is part of the Christian meaning of marriage.

One way we help each other grow is by giving honest feedback, even if it is painful on both sides. Loving confrontation means mirroring you back to yourself, but at the same time it reveals my dark sides to me. Learning how to communicate feelings, with an honesty which makes me vulnerable, and with a gentleness which respects your feelings, is one of the great arts of married life. The work of years, it is an important part of loving well and calling one another to Christian growth.

5. Gratitude. When we meet and fall in love, we are usually filled with a certain wonder and gratitude for the gift that person is in our life. We are amazed that someone could love us so much, and we appreciate all the things done for us: sending us cards, cooking us meals, helping us with tasks. But the longer we relate to a person, the more easily we take the good things for granted and complain about the bad. The practice makes for painful close relationships. I work several hours to make a special meal. Nothing is said. I burn the meat. You let me know it. You do the laundry and clean the house on your day off. I don't mention it. You come home and watch TV the next evening. I say, "How come all you

ever do is come home and watch TV?" These are the things that crush the human spirit.

An important virtue in marriage is gratitude. It is not just a question of the efforts our partner makes to do something special for us. It is a matter also of the ordinary mutual services of everyday: working to earn money, making the bed, washing dishes, running errands. These need recognition and appreciation too. Taking care to give thanks is one of the ways we love one another in the spirit of Christ.

6. **Dying and Rising.** Frequently in this book we have called attention to another way in which the Gospel message applies to the details of a married couple's life. The death/resurrection experience of Jesus, what we call the paschal mystery, is lived out again and again in our experience. It is the pattern of all life. We die and we rise, and then we die and rise again. Repeatedly we taste the awful ashes of our own dying—the losses, the frustrations, the labors, the sacrifices—and repeatedly we rise again to a life in some way fuller, deeper, richer.

A marriage relationship goes through the process of death/resurrection many times. We give up our unrealistic expectations of one another and of our marriage, and find that this makes possible a life of real love together. We make concessions to each other's ways, sometimes at great personal cost. We take the risk of trying to communicate our feelings to one another, dying to our fears and resistances, and find that new union and understanding arises out of the pain. Our relationship changes and grows, moving through many passages in the course of our lifetime together. It is the only way to the life that lies at more profound levels.

> . . . that I may know him [Jesus] and the power of his resurrection, and may share his sufferings, becoming like

him in his death, that if possible I may attain the resurrection from the dead (*Phil 3:10–11*).

The practice of love necessarily involves Christians in the paschal mystery of Christ, in laying down their lives. This paschal mystery is also a source of hope, when things look bleak, that Christ, by the power of his resurrection, can bring us back to life again.

A friend of ours who is just completing his first two years of marriage summed it up well for us:

> Before Rose and I were married, we said "We've talked about everything; we agree on everything—or at least the major parts. Therefore we're compatible and things will work out accordingly." But then the marriage bliss wears off and the working begins and rebegins, the dying and rising. I doubt that we're emotionally prepared for it.
>
> I think we're in the dark most of the time about what will work and how, and either fearful that we might choose the wrong "strategy" or too ego-centered to care. Learning to deal with the emotions of those situations is really hard.
>
> For me, the way out is to pray to God for guidance in the process, and to listen to his guidance for help. Then it's a matter of being willing to do it faithfully without measuring the personal cost, and to believe that married life is not a series of problems to be solved by our limited wills, but rather a series of growth experiences God leads us through because he loves us and wants us to come to know and trust him through these experiences.

We have looked at some of the ways in which a man and woman become grace for one another. Each reveals God to the other in the way that they love, for God is love. Each is an important, perhaps the most important, channel of grace for the other, for grace is nothing other than God's graciousness to human beings and the transforming effect which that graciousness has upon us when we are open to it. This graciousness of God touches our lives through our partner's faithfulness, forgiveness, generosity, truthfulness, and gratitude. Each of these produces growth and involves us in the paschal mystery of dying and rising.

7. **Outreach to Others.** Not only are a married couple sacrament for one another. The couple, with their children, also show the sacrament to the world. They do this both by living Christian values themselves, and by reaching out to others in need. Every family is called to be open to the needs of the world, to contribute to making our world a more just and loving place. For those couples who do not have children, and even for those who do, this outreach is part of the generativity of marriage.

One value a Christian couple is asked to live is simplicity. Jesus showed a strong concern for simplicity of life, calling attention frequently to the danger of riches. It is easier for a camel to get through the eye of a needle, he said, than for a rich person to enter the kingdom of God (Mk 10:25). This concern of his strikes sharply against the prevalent consumerism and acquisitiveness of Western society. That society tells us that our success as a new couple depends on how quickly we can build up material possessions—house, car, furniture—and establish security through savings and insurance policies. Jesus' concern for simplicity is based not only on the power of riches to take control of our attention and energies. It is also a matter of the needs of our brothers and sisters who lack the means of life.

A couple's concern for others can be expressed in a variety of ways. Hospitality is one of the central New Testament

virtues. The door of the Christian home swings open frequently to outsiders. Church and community call out for
many other services as well. Not only financial resources,
but time, energy, and talents are called forth to meet many
human needs—those of other children, the elderly, refugees,
the poor, the peace movement. Christian love begins at
home, but is as wide as the world itself.

## Prayer and Sacraments

We have said that the Christian life of a married couple
is lived not primarily in church activities, but in the decisions
of daily life. However, prayer and the sacraments are an important part of a Christian marriage too. There are many reasons why this is so.

The kind of love we have described is difficult to sustain. Often culture does not encourage such faithfulness and
generosity. For love to work, a constant tendency toward
selfishness has to be battled with. Prayer and the sacraments
help us keep the Gospel vision alive and strengthen us to
make the choices love demands.

Reading the Bible and praying over passages as a couple
nourishes our life together and keeps the Christian challenge
before us. Regular Sunday worship is also a great help. The
Eucharist has a special power to keep alive the memory of Jesus. It is reminiscent of his whole ministry of table fellowship
with sinners—encounters from which people came away re-
freshed and renewed. Its central symbolism is one of sharing—sharing oneself and all that contributes to life with
others. It symbolizes Jesus' self-sacrifice, his willingness to
spend his life-blood that we might have life and have it more
abundantly (Jn 10:10). It commemorates his death and resurrection as the pattern for human existence. In the Eucharist,
Christ is present as the bread of life, he in us and we in him,

that our life may bear fruit (Jn 15:4–5). The Eucharist strengthens us as married couples to love one another as Jesus has loved us.

So does personal prayer. Today there are more and more books on prayer showing us that there is no one way of doing it, but as many ways as there are persons. One important way is to learn to take the many "natural moments" the day offers and make them times of simple prayer. There are times in the day when the mind is at leisure—as we do the dishes or the laundry, jog or do other exercises, shower and shave, wait in line, drive down the freeway, walk from one place to another, lie in bed waiting for sleep. All of these are moments when we can place ourselves more consciously in God's presence and quietly hold up our lives.

Lifting up a loved one to God is a good way to pray. It can be especially helpful if we are having difficulty knowing how to love that person right now. Or we can simply breathe out the Holy Spirit toward them, wishing them every good. These are both ways of being quietly with someone and loving them in the Lord. We might want to lift up our spouse at times. In fact, the whole world can be brought into our prayer in this way.

There are groups to join for support in prayer. And couples can learn to pray together. Families can pray together for a few minutes before the evening meal. Many families sit and join hands around the table, and each person in turn gives thanks for some blessing of the day or makes a petition. The ways and means of prayer are less important than the fact that a couple find a regular place for it in their life together.

We have tried to show that religion is not something for special times and places in a marriage. God is there right in in the midst of our efforts to comfort and challenge one another every day. "*This* is a holy place—a place of love—and here it is that my temple shall be built." Prayer and the sacraments are necessary supports for our efforts to love, but the heart of our holiness as married people comes from loving one another well, beginning again each day with the determination to follow Jesus' central command: "Love one another as I have loved you."

## EXERCISES

1. Tell each other how you see God in each other. Part of it will be experiences of beauty, goodness, love. Part of it will be experiences of being challenged, stretched, prodded to growth, called into the truth. Reflect on and discuss these things until you begin to get some sense of how God is present and active for you in your partner so that you may have life and have it more abundantly.

2. Share with one another how you want to grow as a Christian, especially in the virtues of a Christian marriage: fidelity to growth, generosity and giftgiving, gratitude, outreach to others, etc. Then state how you would like your mate to help you. Share each in turn, and then discuss, making sure you understand each other.

3. Call to mind the graces that have come to you from the days of your marriage to one another. Then pray a prayer of gratitude together, thanking God for these blessings.

4. Share a simple ritual of forgiveness with one another, using some formula like the following. Each says in turn, "I have hurt you by . . . and I am sorry." The partner replies, "I forgive you as God has forgiven us both."

# Conclusion

A FEW FINAL THOUGHTS.

Trying to make a marriage work, even in the first two years, takes a lot of patience. If at first you don't succeed, try and try again. You cannot get all the wrinkles out of the system at once. Some things probably will not fall into place until some years down the line. Be patient. Don't give up.

Make a commitment to drawing on outside resources to enrich your marriage. Read at least a book a year on some aspect of marriage or of personal growth, and discuss it together. But reading is not enough. It is important to have the experience of being with other couples who are facing difficulties, struggling for growth, and achieving it. Commit yourselves to making a marriage enrichment event with other couples at least once a year. There are many existing programs of quality. If you do not hear of enrichment events being offered in your locality, take your own initiative in making one happen. You are not the only couple who needs it.

We believe in marriage counseling. Many couples shy away from it, thinking they should be able to solve their problems themselves, not wanting to expose their "failure" to anyone else. But the fact is that many times we *cannot* solve our own problems. We are too close to them even to see what they are. We do need outside help, and fortunately the field of marriage and family counseling has come into its own as a separate field of expertise among the mental health professions. When you find yourselves stuck around something, and unable to get the problem dislodged, when you are in pain together and cannot find the way out, seek professional marriage counseling, and do it before it is too late. Sometimes couples wait so long before they seek help that the marriage has died and it is very difficult to bring it back to life. But many a marriage has been saved when couples sought counseling while the problem was still manageable.

Finally, remember that marriage is a fluid reality, like a stream in constant movement. In this book we have focused on the first two years of marriage, offering some perspectives and strategies for laying good foundations. This is important, but it does not guarantee lifetime success. The only thing that guarantees lifetime success is careful attention and constant flexibility. Keep on listening. And keep on adapting to meet the ongoing challenges of all the stages of your married life. The rewards in satisfaction and happiness will more than repay your efforts.

# *Suggestions for Further Reading*

| E. and J. Whitehead | *Marrying Well* | Doubleday, 1981 |
| M. Krantzler | *Creative Marriage* | McGraw-Hill, 1981 |
| J. Powell | *The Secret of Staying in Love* | Argus, 1974 |
| D. and V. Mace | *How To Have a Happy Marriage* | Abingdon, 1977 |
| T. Hart | *Living Happily Ever After: Toward a Theology of Christian Marriage* | Paulist, 1979 |
| D. Briggs | *Celebrate Yourself* | Doubleday, 1977 |
| W. Gaylin | *Feelings* | Ballantine, 1977 |

| | | |
|---|---|---|
| Miller, Nunnally, and Wackmann | *Talking Together* | Interpersonal Communication Programs, 1979 |
| S. Basow | *Sex-Role Stereotypes: Traditions and Alternatives* | Brooks Cole, 1981 |
| M. Kolbenschlag | *Kiss Sleeping Beauty Good-Bye* | Bantam, 1979 |
| G. Augsberger | *Caring Enough To Confront* | Regal, 1973 |
| D. and V. Mace | *Love and Anger in Marriage* | Zondervan, 1982 |
| G. Augsberger | *Caring Enough To Forgive* | Regal, 1981 |
| B. Zilbergeld | *Male Sexuality* | Bantam, 1978 |
| L. Barbach | *For Each Other: Sharing Sexual Intimacy* | Doubleday, 1982 |
| C. and J. Penner | *The Gift of Sex* | Word Books, 1981 |
| D. Briggs | *Your Child's Self-Esteem* | Doubleday, 1970 |
| F. Dodson | *How To Discipline with Love* | Signet, 1977 |
| E. and J. Visher | *How To Win as a Step-Family* | Bantam, 1982 |